FAMILY

JPS Popular Judaica Library
General Editor: Raphael Posner

FAMILY

Edited by Hayyim Schneid

JEWISH PUBLICATION SOCIETY OF AMERICA
Philadelphia, Pa.

First published in Israel by KETER BOOKS, an imprint of
ISRAEL PROGRAM FOR SCIENTIFIC TRANSLATIONS LTD.
P.O. Box 7145, Jerusalem

Published by
THE JEWISH PUBLICATION SOCIETY OF AMERICA
222 N. 15th St., Philadelphia, Pa. 19102

Library of Congress Catalogue Card 73 11760
ISBN 0 8276 0029 1

Printed in Israel

CONTENTS

INTRODUCTION

1. GENEALOGY   1
Brotherhood of Man — In the Bible — Genealogical Records — Scholars and Genealogy — Ten Social Groupings — Honorable Families — Creating a Good Name — Zekhut Avot — Nation of Israel — Charity — Zedakah.

2. FAMILY   10
Family Interrelationships: Husband-Wife — Father-Child — Mother-Child — Brothers — Brother-Sister — The Family Saga: In the Bible — In the Midrash — Legislative Passages — Honor to Parents — Function of Family: Father — Mother — Children and Parents — Children and Children — Jewish Home.

3. PROSELYTES   24
History: In the Bible — The Prototype Convert — Second Temple Period — Talmudic Times — Proselytes by Conviction — Medieval Attitude — 16th Century-Present — Halakhah: Prescribed Ceremonies — State of Israel — Proselyte and Family.

4. BIRTH   33
Pregnancy: Partners in Man — The Fetus — Nine Months — The Ninetieth Day — The Miracle — Determination of Sex — Folklore: Evil Spirits — Amulets — Lilith — Weapons — Naming the Child — Sholem Zokhor — Astrology — Halakhah: Sexual Relations — Sacrifices.

5. ABORTION   46
Birth Pains — Accidental Abortion — Danger to Mother's Life — Law of Pursuer — Without Mortal Danger — Prohibited Unions — Suffering of the Child.

6. CIRCUMCISION   51
History: In the Bible — In the Prophets — Second Temple — Halakhah — The Ceremony: Time — The Sabbath and Festivals — Presenting the Child — Chair of Elijah — The Sandak — The Knife — Periah — Mezizah — Benedictions — Medical Care — Place — In Jewish Thought: Medieval Reasons — Fate — Protection — Reform Judaism — Spinoza.

7. FIRSTBORN   65

Status: *Father's Firstborn – Mother's Firstborn* – In Religion – The Redemption Ceremony: *Time – The Transaction* – Halakhah: *Priests and Levites – Doubtful Primogeniture – Fast of the Firstborn* – Inheritance Rights.

8. ADOPTION   72

In the Bible: *Abraham – Jacob – Moses – Mordecai – Levirate Marriage –* Attitudes: *Maimonides – Charity* – In Law: *Biological Relationship – Guardian – Functions of the Guardian – Inheritance – Naming the Child – Marriage and Divorce* – Problems of Adoption: *Gentile Child – Conversion* – Procedure: *State of Israel – Family Unit.*

9. WOMEN   83

Testimony – Religious Duties – Commandments Based on Time – Benediction – Reading of the Law – Life Cycle Ceremonies – The Homemaker – Study – Divorce – A Midrashic Depiction – Famous Women – State of Israel.

10. THE INTERMEDIATE YEARS   95

Family Education: *In the Bible – Family Interelationships – Ritual –* Method of Instruction: *In the Bible – Second Temple – The Family Experience – Rebellious Son – Parental Harmony – Family Solidarity.*

11. BAR MITZVAH AND BAT MITZVAH   103

Preparation: *Study* – Change of Status: *Puberty* – The Bar Mitzvah Ceremony: *Reading of the Law – Benediction – The Haftarah – Festivities – Discourse – Tefillin* – The Bat Mitzvah Ceremony – Confirmation – Legal Status – The Future.

GLOSSARY

SOURCES

READING LIST

INTRODUCTION

It is conceivable that a society could exist without the family unit; Orwell's book, *1984,* did picture such a society but note that the dictator was called Big Brother. This, however, has hardly happened in history. Indeed, the family unit in slightly varying forms exists in every human society that has been known and even in many species of the animal world. Sociologists have argued as to whether this most common and constant human institution is the result of natural biological instincts or of environmental education. In the light of its universal incidence it would seem that the former view is the more likely, and it was certainly the view of some of the rabbis of the Talmud. For among the very many stories of family life told, there is one about a family in which only one of the sons was legitimate although all of them believed they were. The father left his property to his real son who was identified by a sort of ruse. All the sons were told to beat their father's grave and all did — except one. It was that one whom the rabbis adjudged to be the real son on the theory that there is a biological, instinctive connection between father and son which controls the latter's actions.

Whether "familiness" is an acquired trait or whether it is a deepset natural part of the human being, there is no doubt that the quality of the individual and consequently the quality of society depend, in very large measure, on the quality of the family unit. The Jews have always accepted this thesis as completely beyond discussion, and the striving to create and maintain a good family life has been a constant ideal throughout Jewish history. Life without family is inconceivable in Jewish thought in much the same way as it is impossible to live without breathing. Being a part of a family — taking roles which change in the course of time — is the natural condition of man. Perhaps the best summation is to be found in the biblical verse (Gen. 2:18):

"And the Lord God said: 'it is not good that man should be alone'."

Membership in society is an extension of membership in the immediate family, the former being the equivalent of the clan or tribe of ancient times. The nation is the still wider application, and the utopian ideal is membership in the human family — what has been called "the brotherhood of man." The sense of belonging to the wider families, however, will never be achieved unless the primary unit is understood and appreciated.

This book, which follows *Marriage* in the Popular Judaica Library, tells about the family in all its many and varied aspects. It discussess genealogy and the various family interrelationships as they are in the Bible, rabbinic literature and modern life. It also discusses family events such as birth, circumcision, namegiving and confirmation. Together with *Age and the Aged* which is forthcoming, these books will complete the story of the life cycle of the Jew.

As in the other books of this series, the aim is to put the basic material before the reader who, we hope, will be enticed to read more on the subject and ultimately form his own conclusions.

Coat of arms of the De Worms family of England.

1. GENEALOGY

'All Israelites are mutually accountable for each other.' In a boat at sea one of the men began to bore a hole in the bottom of the boat. On being remonstrated with, he answered: 'I am only boring under my own seat.' 'Yes', said his comrades, 'but when the sea rushes in we shall all be drowned with you.' So it is with Israel. Its weal or its woe is in the hands of every individual Israelite.

Midrash

All men are God's children and thus all men are brothers. The *Brotherhood* sages of the Mishnah nearly two thousand years ago stressed this *of Man* doctrine in their own way by asking, why, when God created the human being, did He not create several men and women at the same time, or at least a pair, just as the animals had been created? Why did he interrupt the pattern of creation by creating a single Adam, and only later, after realizing His "mistake", continue with the creation of Eve? Furthermore, why was it necessary to create woman out of the existing man, and not to create her in the same manner as He had created him? The explanation, as recorded in the Mishnah, points to the divine desire to demonstrate the brotherhood of man. Everyone, no matter what his culture or religion, no matter if he be a king or a beggar, is descended from one root. No man may say, "My ancestor was greater than yours."

Most people, however, are unable to feel this universality of man. Except for a gifted few, the human being feels no loyalty beyond his loyalty to country, clan and family. The basic unit, the family, should educate a person to extend his acquired reactions outside his immediate group.

In every family, obviously, genealogy plays a part. In the many genealogical lists found in the Bible, one common feature is apparent and sheds light on the ancient structure of society. In every group, whether national, tribal, or familial, each individual member is descended from a common father. In order for an individual to associate with the clan, he would, therefore, need to prove his connection with some ancient ancestor of the group. Only in this manner could an individual claim the privileges of citizen status. Thus, even today, the words "son (or daughter) of Abraham", are added to the new Hebrew name given to an individual who converts to Judaism. In this manner, he establishes a direct genealogical link with the founder of the Jewish people. This association serves as testimony that he, just as those who have been born Jewish, is a member of the Jewish nation.

Historically, the Jewish people have attached varied degrees of importance to genealogy. Until the destruction of the First Temple in 586 b.c.e., possession of a family or clan genealogical

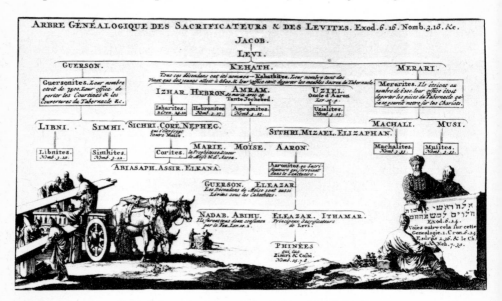

Copper plate engraving of the genealogy of the Tribe of Levi, beginning with the Patriarch Jacob. The engraving is from the French work *République des Hébreux* by Jacques Basnage, Amsterdam, 1713.

list was an asset, though in most cases not necessary. It was not difficult to establish ownership of property or membership in the priestly clan, because the tribes lived in relatively settled times. Even with the division of the nation into two kingdoms, after the times of King Solomon (10th century b.c.e.), it remained a fairly simple task to reconstruct one's ancestry. However, with the destruction of the Temple in 586 b.c.e. and the mass movement of a great segment of the populace to centers outside Israel, it became necessary, especially for priests who would someday return and resume their function in a newly built Temple, to record their ancestry as proof of their rightful privileges. The necessity for documentation was by no means confined to priests. Returning families, wishing to reclaim ancestral holdings, had a similar need for proof. The division of the kingdom into twelve tribal territories, at one time simplifying the tribal tradition, had broken down. Intermarriage between tribes and movement of peoples obscured that tradition until it was unrecognizable. Furthermore, until Ezra (one of the leaders of the return to Zion in the sixth century b.c.e.) had abolished all foreign marriages with heathens, a new unknown element had emerged amidst the people. To sort out the lineage and extract or discard the alien elements was a difficult task; proper identification for future generations could only be assured by accurate and systematic preservation of genealogical lists.

Notwithstanding the great effort to do so, it is easily understandable why the task of keeping genealogical records met with only partial success. It was for this reason that centuries later the scholars of the Talmud, undoubtedly with regret, found it necessary to devote folio upon folio to the problems of lineage presented by the destruction of the Temple, exile, return to Erez Israel, and ensuing confusion which was to affect the people for generations and centuries.

During the Second Temple period (fifth century b.c.e.—first century c.e.) purity of descent played an important role in the life of the people. Besides the individual families that kept records, a general genealogical list of priests was maintained in the Temple compound. Even priests living in the Diaspora supplied the necessary information to the Temple record keepers.

It is important to note, however, that the religious leaders of the people achieved their positions of influence irrespective of their descent. Some sages, it is true, were of noble descent, but others came from families with no genealogical record, and there were even a few who were the descendants of proselytes. Indeed, the Talmud records the gentile origins of some sages, including some of the greatest, such as Akiva and Meir; some sages were even reputed to have descended from infamous and evil families. Furthermore, a bastard, one of the lowest ranking individuals in society, could attain a higher status than a priest for, as the Mishnah states, "a learned bastard takes precedence over an uneducated High Priest." The evident purpose of such accounts and of such legislation was to demonstrate that Torah learning and piety were not dependent on family background and were more important than it.

After the destruction of the Second Temple in 70 c.e., when the priests lost their function, they prized their purity of descent even more, for it was the last symbol left to them of their exalted status. However, with the passage of time, they too could not document their past.

Many developments testify to the degeneration of the concept of genealogy. For example, the Mishnah lists ten social groups which returned from Babylonia with Ezra. They are, in order of their genealogical precedence: 1) *Priests* — male descendants of Moses' brother, Aaron, who was High Priest during the Israelite sojourn in the wilderness after the Exodus from Egypt; 2) *Levites* — male descendants of the tribe of Levi; 3) *Israelites* — all other Jews of umblemished heritage; 4) *Ḥalalim* — offspring of forbidden marriages entered into by priests; they were not permitted to marry with the priests and counted as "ordinary"

4

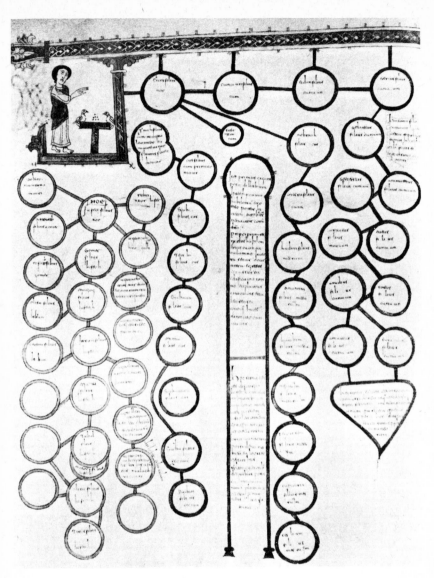

Part of a "Table of Nations." The nations of the world — traditionally there are 70 — are classified as descended from one or another of Noah's three sons. From a Latin Manuscript completed in Zamora, Northern Spain, 975 c.e. In the upper left hand corner, Noah is shown offering a sacrifice after the Flood.

5

Israelites; 5) *Gerim* — converts to Judaism, who are equal to Israelites, except that they may enter certain marriages prohibited to Israelites; 6) *Ḥarurim* — freed slaves; 7) *Mamzerim* — i.e., bastards, the children of prohibited unions and their offspring who may only marry other *mamzerim* or *gerim;* 8) *Netinim* — the descendants of the Gibbeonites who were circumcised at the time of Joshua and were not regarded as full Jews because their conversion was effected by trickery; 9) *Shetukim* — persons unable to identify their father; and 10) *Asufim* — persons unable to identify either their father or mother. Not included in the scale are gentiles and slaves, who have no legal status at all, but who, upon conversion or being set free, began their own genealogies. The relationships among the groups are discussed in the Talmud, although by the fifth—sixth centuries c.e., when the Talmud was completed, not all groupings or even members of groups could be identified. For example, descendants of *mamzerim* although themselves *mamzerim,* could no longer be singled out after only a couple of generations. Thus, the practical application of the talmudic discussions could only be partially effective.

Although the Talmud does make reference to honorable families and individuals, their honorable status is often a result of their behavior and attitudes, not their lineage. For example, the Talmud states, "Anyone with a family stigma stigmatizes others, and never praises anyone." An implication of this dictum is that a person who always degrades others must come from a lower class; his behavior determines his position. Similarly, it is said, "When two people quarrel one sees which person becomes silent first and says of him, 'This one is of superior birth'." Hence, the emphasis is on upbringing; the accident of birth is not considered a very important criterion. However, birth was not to be disregarded altogether: "When the Holy One causes His Divine Presence to rest, it is upon Israelite families of pure birth." The sages further taught, "The Holy One is reluctant to uproot a

Honorable Families

6

name from a place in a genealogical tree," and objected to "anyone taking a wife not fit for him" because he disregarded the importance of birth. Although it was stressed that a family once absorbed into the community is not to be excluded (even if a stigma was discovered in its genealogy), a man should still be careful not to marry into a family to which a stigma had been attached even in the distant past. As a rule, however, people were instructed not to reveal the truth concerning families whose stigma had been generally forgotten.

Except in Hasidism, in which descent from the *zaddik* is endowed with special significance because it is believed that the *zaddik* transmits some of his sanctity to his descendants, the idea of status by birth has all but disappeared. Many medieval and modern rabbis have stressed the value of a man creating his own good name. However, even nowadays, in some circles, emphasis is placed on family background, especially when it comes to finding a marriage partner. This consideration is known as *yiḥus*. *Creating a Good Name*

Genealogy, however, is involved in an important theological concept. There is a doctrine in Judaism of *zekhut avot* ("merit of the fathers"), which teaches that progeny benefit from the righteous acts of their forbears. This concept is mentioned often in the Bible and throughout rabbinic literature in relation to the Patriarchs Abraham, Isaac and Jacob, and in some sources to the Matriarchs Sarah, Rebekah, Rachel and Leah. The doctrine has been repeatedly applied to Israel, who may receive God's favorable attention even at a time when they are undeserving, as the righteous deeds of the "fathers" are still remembered by Him. *Zekhut Avot*

On this concept Solomon Levy wrote, "Judaism insists that man has an inborn impulse to virtue ('Original Virtue') which can overcome all temptation to sin; an impulse immeasurably strengthened through the 'merit of the fathers' which is accounted unto their children as righteousness. That man is best able to advance on the road to moral perfection who starts with the accumulated spritual heritage of righteous ancestors."

7

In a delightful twist, Israel Abrahams describes the concept: "The old Jewish doctrine of the 'merit of the fathers' has a counterpart — the idea that the righteousness of the living child favorably affects the fate of the dead father. This might be called the doctrine of the 'merit of the children'. In this way the living and the dead hold converse. The real message of the dead is — their virtue. The real response of the living is again — their virtue. This is a bridge built over the chasm of the tomb. Thus do the hearts of the fathers and children beat in eternal unison."

A very important consequence of the sense of genealogy is *Nation of Is* that the nation of Israel, in many ways, behaves as a family unit. Tragedies affect not only the immediate family but the entire nation. This has been true throughout the ages and is evident even in modern times. Whereas, President Anwar Sadat of Egypt can claim that his country and its allies are prepared to sacrifice millions of lives in a holy war against Israel, Israel has difficulty absorbing the loss of even one life as it brings personal grief to each and every individual. Israel's Prime Minister, Golda Meir, immediately after the exchange of war prisoners between Israel and Syria in 1973, expressed the national feeling of joy when she said that her gladness was enhanced by knowing that many Syrian and Lebanese families — wives, children and parents — could rejoice, after an unfortunately long period of absence, at the return of their loved ones.

This national family bond is clearly expressed in the practical *Charity* act of giving charity. In Judaism, charity is a religious precept which demands extreme care and diligence in its fulfillment. Far more than being an act of grace, charity between man and man is the main foundation of the united people of Israel. As the ancient adage has it, "All Israelites are mutually accountable for each other."

The Hebrew word *zedakah* expressed this idea since it means *Zedakah* both justice and charity, the two concepts being one and the same in Jewish teaching. Man is not given the choice to be or not

8

to be charitable, for just as he is enjoined to be just, so must he be charitable. After the performance of charitable acts, one should not say, "I have dealt with my fellow man benevolently," but rather, "I have dealt with my fellow man justly, as I must do."

Therefore, a man is required to relate to others in the same way as he deals with his family, for just as he is required to clothe his children so is he required to clothe his brethren. Just as his dealings with his family are not in the realm of charity, so too are his dealings with mankind. Obviously, one's obligations begin with the closest to him, his family and kin, but it was never meant to end there. He must treat all mankind with justice, beginning with the needy of his city and country, even to include his non-Jewish neighbors and those in the remotest parts of the universe.

A Bene Israel family, c. 1890. The Bene Israel are Indian Jews who claim to have been on Indian soil since the second century b.c.e. Most are now living in Israel.

*Now the Lord said unto Abram: '. . . I will make of thee
a great nation, and I will bless thee, and make thy name
great; and be thou a blessing: And I will bless them that
bless thee, and him that curseth thee will I curse; and in
thee shall all the families of the earth be blessed.*

Genesis

"The Jew's home has rarely been his 'castle'. Throughout the
ages it has been something far higher — his sanctuary." In the
Bible, all aspects of home life are apparent. Included among them
are love and respect of the spouses, love for children, respect for
parents, and sibling rivalry together with brotherly love. The
family values as they have developed throughout the ages are
already clear in the biblical narratives.

Family Interrelationships
The main characteristic of the husband-wife relationship even
from the earliest times, has been mutual devotion and respect.
Several biblical accounts stressing the suffering of barren women
are accompanied by descriptions of their husbands' compassion.
One such story is told of Elkanah whose wife, Hannah, refused to
accept the gifts he had given her, deeming herself unworthy of
them because she was unable to bear him a child. Elkanah
responded that even her giving birth to ten children could not
compare with,or replace the love between them.

Loyalty of spouses is also evident in many of the narratives.
Michal, King Saul's daughter and the future King David's wife,
demonstrated her loyalty to her husband by deceiving her
father's messengers, who had been sent to murder David. By the

Husband-W

10

Elkanah and his family (I Samuel 1) from the *Bible Historiée Le Roy* Lyons, 1479(?). The unhappy childless Hannah must take second place to the gloating Peninah and Elkanah is embarrassed.

time the messengers had discovered her deceit, David had escaped.

The interrelationship of father and child in the Bible, is one of respect and love. When the sons of Jacob went down to Egypt to procure food for their father, in Canaan, the youngest among them, Benjamin, was placed in prison. The brothers, realizing that they could not return to their father without Benjamin, pleaded for his release, on the grounds that Jacob's fatherly love for the child was such that his absence would in his words, "... bring down my grey hairs with sorrow to the grave." Unbeknown to them, this passionate plea was made to Joseph, the brother whom they had sold into slavery many years earlier. Moved by their words, Joseph discloses his identity: "And Joseph could no longer contain himself... and he began to

Father-Child

11

weep . . . and he said 'I am Joseph. Does my father still live?'"
Before all else, Joseph inquires as to his father's health.

Rashi, the medieval commentator, added a new dimension to the biblical story of the *Akedah* ("Binding of Isaac") emphasizing every single word for additional familial significance. The story, in essence deals with Abraham's obedience to God, but is expanded to deal with the interpersonal feelings of father and son. When Abraham and Isaac are on the last leg of the journey and nearing the chosen place at which Abraham was to sacrifice his son, the narrative repeats itself: "and they both went together." At first, only Abraham knew of the impending sacrifice, and although deeply troubled by it because of his love of Isaac, he was able to walk as Isaac walked, willingly, as if he felt nothing. Later, after Isaac had asked his father, "Where is the

sheep for the slaughter?", and from Abraham's response he understood that it was he himself who would be the victim, the narrative repeats, "and they both went together". Because of his respect for his father, Isaac was able to proceed in a similar spirit, willingly and with joy.

Joseph. on the throne, receives his brothers. In the center is Benjamin, the youngest of them. This is one of ten ivory panels from the "Throne of Maximian" in Ravenna (opposite). King Solomon judging the disputed maternity of the baby, from a 13th century English Psalter (right).

The mother is depicted, in the Bible, as having unlimited compassion for her children. When King Solomon sat in judgment over the disputed maternity of an infant child, he devised a trick which played on the mother's compassion. He ordered the infant cut into two pieces, one half to be given to each woman. The true mother revealed herself when she stated her preference for the child to be given to the other rather than see its death.

Mother-Child

13

Brothers are seen as rivals as well as caring relatives. Jacob *Brothers*
and Esau vie for parental love and even prepare for battle against
each other. However, at the last moment, brotherly love prevails
and a confrontation is avoided. Similarly, Joseph's jealous
brothers intend to kill him, but the eldest, Reuben, averts the
danger and, as a delaying measure, has Joseph thrown into a pit,
hoping to save him and return him to their father.

Sisters and brothers are usually depicted as protecting one *Brother-Sister*
another. Thus Miriam protects her brother Moses after he has
been placed in a basket and set afloat on the Nile. So too,
Dinah's brothers avenge her seduction by the prince Shechem, by
destroying him and his community.

Two sections of the mosaic in the Monreale Cathedral, Sicily, showing epi-
sodes from the life of the Patriarch Isaac. On the left Isaac bids Esau hunt
for food as Rebekah eavesdrops. On the right, Jacob, on Rebekah's instructions, deceives his father and receives the blessing in Esau's place.

14

The Family Saga

The entire book of Genesis is really the saga of a family. We read *In the Bible* of Abraham and Sarah, together with the complications of Abraham's concubine Hagar, and later in relation with their son Isaac; Isaac and his relationship with his wife Rebekah, and his two sons, Jacob and Esau, and in turn the brothers' relationship; Jacob and his family, and especially the stories of the twelve brothers. The other books of the Bible do not contain as many family stories, although there are glimpses of family settings, for example, Moses with his brother, Aaron, and his sister, Miriam, as well as with his wife, Zipporah, his sons, and his father-in-law. Other instances can be cited, such as Samuel, the monarchs, Caleb, Gideon and Samson.

Midrashic and talmudic literature are replete with stories of *In the Midrash* the family. The Talmud tells us of Rachel, the daughter of a wealthy Jerusalemite, who was disowned by her father when she married Akiva, a poor shepherd. The couple was subject to extreme poverty, and in order to eat, Rachel was forced to sell her hair. She was prepared to endure these hardships in order that Akiva could begin to study Torah. Akiva later became the leading scholar of his day and one of the greatest sages in Jewish history. His love for Rachel is reflected in his saying, "Who is wealthy? . . . He who has a wife comely in deeds."

Another story is told of Beruryah, the wife of Rabbi Meir. The Midrash relates that when two of her sons died on a Sabbath, she did not inform Meir of their children's death upon his return from the academy, in order not to grieve him on the Sabbath. Only after dark on Saturday night did she broach the matter, saying, "Some time ago a certain man came and left something in my trust; now he has called for it. Shall I return it to him or not? " "Naturally," Meir replied, whereupon Beruryah showed him their dead sons. When Meir began to weep, she asked: "Did you not tell me that we must give back what is given in trust? 'The Lord has given, and the Lord has taken away.' "

15

God commanding Abraham to sacrifice his son Isaac (above) and Abraham
informs his wife Sarah (below). Although the biblical narrative makes no
mention of Abraham telling Sarah, according to the Midrash, the news
reached her indirectly, after Abraham and Isaac began the journey, and she
died of shock. The page is from the Queen Mary Psalter, 14th century.

The concept of the Jewish family is given further expression *Legislative*
in the strictly legislative passages of the Bible. For example, a list *Passages*
is given of the blood relatives with whom a man may not marry,

thus differentiating between a sound family structure and promiscuous relationships. The same distinction emerges from another passage, which describes the ritual process for testing a woman suspected by her husband of infidelity. Several passages discuss the inheritance rights of daughters in the absence of a male heir. The procedure for divorce is briefly mentioned and a military exemption for a new bridegroom is prescribed. Should a husband die childless, the Bible relates the obligation of his brother towards his widow, i.e., to marry her, enabling her to have children so that the dead man's name will be carried on. Several of the commandments in the Decalogue deal with aspects of the family, for example, "Honor thy father and thy mother" and "Thou shalt not commit adultery."

The rabbis of the Talmud, as well, discussed these legislative matters and often explained them with analogous stories. The obligation of honoring one's parents, for example, is explained in a charming talmudic passage. Dama, a non-Jew of Ashkelon, who owned certain precious stones, was visited by officials from the Temple in Jerusalem who wanted to purchase them for the High Priest's breastplate. Dama, however, refused their offer of 600,000 gold coins, because the key to his jewel case was under the pillow on which his father lay sleeping. His reward was not long in coming. A red heifer, of the rare kind sought for the purification ritual in the Temple, was born in his herd. Once again the officials called upon him, this time to purchase the heifer. Anticipating their proposal, Dama said: "I know that if I ask you for all the money in the world you will be willing and ready to pay it. I only ask that you pay me the same sum I lost in the performance of the command to honor my father." This he said, lest he profit by observing the precept of parental honor.

Function of Family

Aside from the interrelationships of members of the family in the biblical scheme, each person had a function to fill insofar as

"An Old Jew with Children" by Kramsztyck, Warsaw, 1942. This was a common ghetto scene (left). "Isaac Blessing Jacob," ink wash drawing by Rembrandt (below).

family organization was concerned. The father was the head of the family unit and owner of its property, and the family was aptly termed *bet av* ("house of the father"). He was the chief authority of the household. Though a man left his parents when he married, he normally remained a member of his father's family. In relation to his wife, he was "master" *(ba'al).* He "took" her away from her parents, or she was "given" to him by her father, or by her master or mistress, if she was a slave, or by both her parents. The marriage negotiations might result from an attraction that had already developed between two young people, but generally the father must have taken the initiative since he had the right to determine the daughter's spouse.

Ideally the husband was expected to be benevolent, to show both love and pity to his family. The patriarchal blessing evidently carried legal force with regard to the distribution of the patrimony and other attendant privileges.

The modern definitions of monogamy and polygamy are not strictly applicable to the ancient world. It was normal for the head of a household to have only one legal, full-fledged wife; if she were barren, the husband had the right to take a concubine who was often the wife's maid. However, a man might take two wives of equal standing. Strict monogamy seems to have been more commonplace than either of the other arrangements.

The mother, if she were the senior wife of a polygamous *Mother* marriage or the sole wife of a monogamous marriage, occupied a place of honor and authority, in spite of her subordination to her husband. The wife, living with her husband, was part of her husband's family circle. Occasions when the groom stayed with the bride's parents are noted in the Bible, perhaps precisely because they were not the norm. Heroic figures such as Moses and Jacob were forced because of unusual circumstances to spend long periods with their in-laws.

When her father died, a woman's brother would perform all the fatherly duties, such as choosing a husband, and providing

19

and caring for her welfare. Thus, before marriage, a girl was under her father's care and after marriage, her husband's. Only in rare instances did a woman become the head of a household and leader of a family. At her husband's death the wife might become the actual, and probably the legal, head of the household, if there were no sons of responsible age. As a widow she was especially vulnerable to oppression and, therefore, concern for her welfare was deemed a measure of good government and of a wholesome society. The influence of famous mothers, such as Sarah and the wife of Manoah, illustrates the significance attached to their role. Not all of their power was exercised openly; often the motherly strategm is deemed worthy of special notice. The stratagems of Rebekah who secured the fatherly blessing for her son Jacob, Leah who expected a favor from her sister, and Rachel who stole the household idols from her father's house are examples. The mother naturally displayed care and love for her husband and offspring.

According to the Talmud, children are a divine trust. It is the father's duty to teach his child the precepts of religion, a trade, and even how to swim. It is strictly forbidden for a parent to show any favoritism to any of his children; the dire consequences of Jacob's favoring Joseph are pointed to by the rabbis as an object lesson in this regard. Domestic harmony is implied in the talmudic injunction: "A man should spend less than his means on food, up to his means on clothes, but beyond his means in honoring his wife and children, because they are dependent on him."

Children and Parents

The talmudic attitude towards children is based on that of the Bible, which teaches that the greatest misfortune that can befall a couple is childlessness. Children are a blessing from the Almighty and they assure the continuance of the family name. Historically, the mother was more directly involved in the early training of the children than was the father. When the children grew older, the father assumed responsibility for instructing the

"Seder" by Eva Meitner, a child in the Theresienstadt concentration camp, 1943.

son, while the mother evidently kept charge of the daughter until marriage. Children are exhorted to honor both parents. "Honor thy father and thy mother, in order that thou shalt lengthen thy days upon the earth that God has given thee." Perhaps the verse is not meant as a warning with an accompanying punishment, i.e., Honor . . . or else . . .; "in order" may rather refer to the logical sequence of events. He who does not honor his parents brings about the destruction of the family, and thus the family's days are numbered. The inclusion of this commandment in the Decalogue testifies to its importance in shaping not only the family, but with it the clan, tribe, and nation. Thus the prophets speak of the decline in the respect due to parents as symptomatic of the dissolution of society. "In thee have they made light of father and mother; in the midst of thee have they dealt by

21

oppression with the stranger; in thee have they wronged the fatherless and the widow." Demonstration of this respect was primarily through obedience. Parental control included the right to sell daughters in marriage, although there were limitations on selling her into slavery, and an absolute ban on selling her for prostitution. The father could annul his daughter's vows, and damages were paid to him for a wrong done to her. A daughter who was widowed or divorced might return to her father's household.

The terms "brother" and "sister" *(ah* and *ahot)* applied both to offspring who had the same father and mother as well as to offspring who had only one common parent. Attempts have been made to find traces in the ancient Israelite tradition of a fratri-archal system in which the brother, not the father, is the household head. Examples, such as Laban's role as head of the family when his sister Rebekah was sent to marry Isaac, or the role of Dinah's brothers, are cited in support of this theory. Whether or

Children and
Children

A silver bound prayer book from Italy, 17th century, The medallion of the Levi family appears on both front and rear covers.

not a fratriarchy existed, the brother's function is an important one, and not only in relation to his sisters. Brotherly solidarity is frequently stressed in the Bible and harmony among brothers was held up as an ideal. In the words of the Psalmist, "Behold how good and pleasant it is for brethren to dwell together." This ideal has legal consequences. Brothers were not only expected, but obligated to avenge each other's murder and to ransom a brother taken captive.

The term "brother" is often extended to more distant relatives, e.g. nephews, fellow tribesmen, and even to include the descendants of Esau and the Edomites.

"Spinoza" by S. Hirszenberg, depicting Spinoza after his excommunication. Excommunication was considered one of the gravest punishments as it meant that the individual was completly isolated. Note the Jews in the background keeping their distance.

Jewish Home

The constant insistence upon the value of the family as a social unit for the propagation of domestic and religious virtues has had the result of making the Jewish home the most vital factor in the survival of Judaism and the preservation of the Jewish way of life, much more than any other Jewish institutions, even the synagogue and the school. Perhaps in nothing can the strength of the family bond be seen better than in the paradox that whereas in theory divorce among Jews is an easy process, in practice it was, until recent times, a comparative

23

rarity. The powerful family bond with mutual responsibilities and considerations made the home a bulwark of Judaism able to withstand all stresses from without and from within.

In describing the Jewish ghetto, David Philipson wrote, "In the narrow lanes and by-ways of the old Jewish quarter of many a European town there grew up that beautiful Jewish home-life which, though its story is seldom recorded, is more important than the outer events and misfortunes that historians have made note of. And as we look upon the unsightly houses, the wretched exterior seems to float away and the home-scenes of joy and love and religious constancy shine brilliantly forth — perpetual lamps — and explain how, in spite of woe and misery such as have fallen to the lot of no other people, the Jews have found strength to live and hope on."

3. PROSELYTES

Your question, why I do not try to make converts, has, I must say, somewhat surprised me. The duty to proselytize springs clearly from the idea that outside a certain belief there is no salvation. I, as a Jew, am not bound to accept that dogma, because, according to the teachings of the Rabbis, 'the righteous of all nations shall have a part in the rewards of the future world.' Your motive, therefore, is foreign to me; nay, as a Jew, I am not allowed publicly to attack any religion which is sound in its moral teachings.

Moses Mendelssohn
To a non-Jewish correspondent

The Jewish nation is, as we have seen, something of an enlarged family group with all its members being able to trace their

"The Circumcision of Isaac," detail from a full page miniature of the *Regensburg Pentateuch*, Germany, c. 1300. The scene proceeds from right to left: Sarah (in the red cloak) accompanied by her servants is holding the baby Isaac. On the left, the *sandak* is seen holding Isaac, while Abraham performs the circumcision. Both Abraham and the *sandak* are wearing the medieval German Jewish hats.

A circumcision ceremony at Moshav Ramot Me'ir in Israel, 1972.

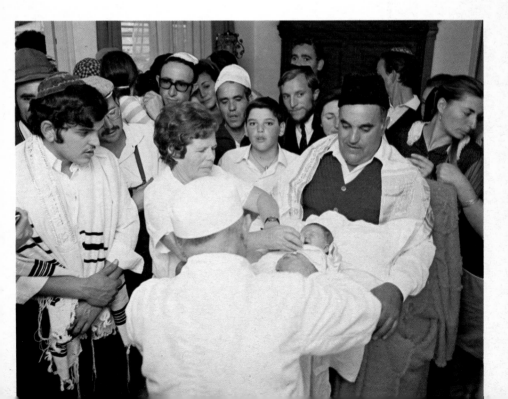

A Torah wrapper, made from
the diaper on which a baby has been
circumcised. This linen wrapper is
from South Germany, 1715, and is
embroidered in silk thread.

Ritual circumcision implements.
Silver and amber knife with
inscription on the blade, Near
East, 1819. Silver foreskin bowl,
Germany, 18th century. Silver
bottle, Italy, 18th-19th century.
Silver protective shield, France,
19th century. They are set
against a book of laws and
prayers for circumcision by
Jacob Sofer ben Judah Loeb
of Berlin, Germany, 1729.

descent from one common ancestor. In this scheme of things there is no place for the outsider. However, the Jewish nation is not just an ethnic group but also a body with a definite belief and religion which it sees as one of its aims to propogate. Thus the proselyte, i.e. the person who subscribes to Judaism's beliefs and wants to be a part of it, is — in a sense — adopted into the family. Every born Jew has kith and kin as long as there is another born Jew alive. The proselyte, while being accepted into the wider family has no such relatives until he creates them himself; he begins his genealogy and his children will be his kith and kin.

Ruth the Moabite with her husband's kinsman, Boaz, who later married her. From a 16th century engraving.

History

The term *Ger* (literally "stranger") was used from Second Temple times for converts to Judaism. In the Bible, however, it was generally used for resident aliens, i.e., non-Jews who lived permanently among the tribes of Israel. These aliens did not convert to Judaism although they were subject to some of the commandments, such as the prohibition against idolatry. In return, the alien could expect to enjoy many of the citizenship privileges, such as equal treatment before the law, the right to eat of the fallen fruit of the tree or of the grain stalks accidentally left beind in the fields by the reapers. After having lived among the tribes for three generations, Egyptians and Edomites were permitted to intermarry with Israelite women, although the same privilege was not afforded to the Moabite and Ammonite men. In the latter case, even after ten generations the prohibition of inter-marriage existed. The resident aliens' status, as opposed to that of foreigners who lived amongst the Jews on a more temporary basis, was geared to assimilate them culturally and, possibly later, religiously into the Jewish nation.

The Bible speaks of several resident aliens who became pros-elytes and consequently subjected themselves to the entire spectrum of the *halakhah,* and who became an integral part of the nation. Perhaps the most outstanding example is Ruth the Moabite who later was considered the prototype of the religious convert. After her husband's death, her mother-in-law, Naomi, bade her to remain amongst the Moabites while she, Naomi, returned to her people. Ruth replied: "Entreat me not to leave thee, to remain behind; whither thou goest, I will go; where thou lodgest, I will lodge; thy people will be my people; thy God shall be my God; where thou shalt die, I too shall die, and there will I be buried . . . " This is one of the most beautiful statements of love and devotion in the entire Bible. The Midrash amplifies it to include religious intent and explains that when Naomi told Ruth to remain behind because Jewish women do not frequent

26

theaters and circuses, she replied, "Whither thou goest, I will go"; when informed that Jewish women only dwell in houses sanctified by *mezuzot,* she responded, "Where thou lodgest, I will lodge"; "Thy people will be my people" revealed her intent to give up idolatry and, "Thy God shall be my God" was Ruth's ultimate wish that God judge her accordingly, returning reward if it was due. Her righteousness and sincerity were amply rewarded, and her great-grandson, David, became the most beloved king of Israel.

Whereas, there is no evidence of widespread conversion to Judaism in the Bible, there is ample evidence that many conversions occurred during the Second Temple period, and in one instance an entire nation, the Idumeans, was forced to accept Judaism. This mass conversion took place during the reign of John Hyrcanus (135—104 b.c.e.) and within a few generations an Idumean became king of the Jews. It is clear, therefore, that proselytes were overwhelmingly accepted into the fold, although, in this particular case, the king, Herod I (37—4 b.c.e.) brought shame and discredit to the Jews, thus alienating many co-religionists. To label Herod a "butcher" would be mild, for he killed several of his own sons and wives. Emperor Augustus is said to have commented, "It is better to be Herod's pig than his son", the former having better chances of survival. Herod, and others like him caused negative attitudes towards proselytes from time to time, but for the most part a favorable attitude prevailed. *Second Temple Period*

The talmudic attitude, representing the second through the fifth centuries c.e., was usually positive. When Aquila the Proselyte inquired: "Is this all the love which the Lord hath given unto the proselyte, as it is written (in Deuteronomy), 'He (God) loveth the stranger (proselyte) to give him bread and clothing', Rabbi Joshua explained: "Bread means Torah . . .; clothing means the *tallit* (fringed garment); the man who is worthy to have the Torah, will also acquire its precepts; his daughters may marry into the priesthood and their grandsons will sacrifice burnt *Talmudic Times* offerings on the altar," a function reserved for the elite. Rabbi Simeon speaks of the proselyte in an even more loving tone: "It is written (in Judges), 'and those that are beloved by Him are compared to the sun when it rises in all its strength': Now who is greater, he who loves the king, or he whom the king loves? One must say, he whom the king loves, as the verse says: 'He (God) loves the stranger (proselyte)'." Furthermore, it was taught, "Proselytes are beloved; in every place He (God) considers them as part of Israel." Rabbi Eleazar said: "Whoever befriends a proselyte is considered as if he created him." During the talmudic period, the benediction for the welfare of the righteous and the pious in the silent prayer *(amidah),* was expanded to include proselytes.

The Rothschild family coat of arms granted by the Austrian College of Heralds in 1822.

However, the high regard afforded proselytes applied only to those who converted out of religious conviction. Because of many bitter experiences with proselytes, many an admirer of proselytes ended by cursing the insincere convert. Thus, Rabbi Nehemiah taught: "Proselytes who converted in order to marry, or converted to enjoy the royal table, or to become a servant of Solomon, proselytes who converted from fear . . ., proselytes who converted because of a dream, are not acceptable as pros-

Proselytes by Conviction

elytes, unless they convert (as) at the present time," i.e., out of conviction, in times when the Jewish people suffer political decline, oppression, persecution; when there can be no material benefit. Rabbi Hiyya took a hard line against all proselytes: "Do not have any faith in a proselyte until twenty-four generations have passed because the inherent evil is still within him." Other rabbis blamed the proselytes who left Egypt with Moses for making the Golden Calf.

However, the predominant view was expressed by Maimonides, the great scholar of the 12th century, who addressed a letter to Obadiah the Proselyte, permitting him to pray:

> "... as every native Israelite prays and recites benedictions ... Anyone who becomes a proselyte and anyone who believes in the unity of God as it is written in the Torah, is a pupil of our father Abraham and all of them are members of his household ... Hence you may say, Our God, and the God of our Fathers; for Abraham, peace be upon him, is your father ... for since you have entered beneath the wings of the Divine Presence and attached yourself to Him, there is no difference between us and you ... You may certainly recite the blessings: 'Who has chosen us', 'Who has caused us to inherit', and 'Who has separated us'. For the Creator has already chosen you and has separated you from the nations and has given you the Torah, as the Torah was given to us and to proselytes ... Further, do not belittle your lineage: Whereas we trace our descent to Abraham, Isaac, and Jacob, your connection is with Him by Whose word the universe came into being."

Furthermore, Maimonides wrote:

> "Toward father and mother we are commanded to show honor and reverence, toward the prophets to obey them, but toward the proselytes we are commanded to have great love

in our innermost hearts . . . God, in His glory, loves proselytes . . . A man who leaves his father and birthplace and the realm of his people at a time when they are powerful, who understands with his insight, and who attaches himself to this nation which today is a despised people, the slave of rulers, and recognizes and knows that their religion is true and righteous . . . and pursues God . . . and enters beneath the wings of the Divine Presence . . . , the Lord does not call you fool, but intelligent and understanding, wise and walking correctly, a pupil of Abraham our father . . . "

With the Expulsion from Spain in 1492 and with the beginnings of Lutheranism, a mostly negative approach to proselytism developed. The Jews were, in many countries, prohibited from practicing active proselytization. They were often charged with violating that law and suffered grave consequences. Especially following the Protestant Reformation, when Jews were accused by both the Catholics and the Reformers of every imaginable crime against the battling religions, Jews tried to become inconspicuous, retreating into their own world, allowing the outside to be what it would. Attempts at proselytizing dwindled, although, in countries where freedom of religion was guaranteed, societies for this purpose were formed. Reform Judaism in the United States has maintained that the Jews are obliged to teach their religion to all mankind and to attract like-minded non-Jews into the Jewish community. To implement this, its organization of rabbis established a committee in 1951 to develop "practical means for extending the influence and acceptance of the Jewish religion." The Conservative rabbinate have declined to undertake such efforts, although it accepts prospective converts. The Orthodox rabbinate has remained extremely reluctant to accept converts, making stringent demands on all prospective candidates. These demands, which the Conservative movement also applies, albeit, with less stringency, usually include a good knowledge of the basic tenets of the faith, the dietary laws, and the laws of the Sabbath. It is also held to be desirable that the individual be motivated to convert not for the purposes of marriage or other benefit, but from a sincere desire to be Jewish.

In the State of Israel, the Ministry for Religious Affairs in 1971, established schools at some of the religious kibbutzim, where candidates for conversion undergo an intensive course in Judaism.

Halakhah

Except for Reform Judaism, which stresses that the proselytes *Prescribed* determination to become a Jew and some knowledge of Judaism *Ceremonies* are sufficient for conversion, all other movements require the prescribed talmudic ceremonies, i.e., ritual immersion in a *mikveh* and, for a male, circumcision. When the male has been previously circumcised, blood of the covenant is drawn instead (see page 57). In addition, the proselyte must accept upon himself the obligation to perform the commandments. If the proselyte should refuse to accept these requirements, his conversion will be invalid. According to most authorities, even if the proselyte agrees to fulfill his duties, but, in fact, does not, his conversion will be invalid *post facto*. However, Rabbi Moses Feinstein has suggested that such a conversion might be valid since the lack of knowledge of the commandments does not invalidate a conversion; what would invalidate it is the non-acceptance or lack of observance of the commandments which are known to the convert. Rather ingeniously he has pointed out that although the religious court performing the conversion tells the convert the more important commandments, and although the convert at least verbally accepts what he or she is told, in fact the convert knows that the overwhelming majority of Jews do not observe these duties and believes that the court's standards of observance are in fact unrealistic and not absolutely essential; for otherwise, why do the Jews themselves not adhere to these standards? Thus,

31

Rabbi Feinstein sees the lack of observance as a sort of lack of knowledge and, *post facto,* tends to accept such a convert.

In modern times, especially in the State of Israel, these requirements for conversion have been more and more questioned. It is felt in wide circles that identification with the Jewish people and its fate should constitute sufficient grounds for being considered a Jew; to expect a proselyte to observe the commandments which a majority of born Jews do not keep seems ridiculous. This reasoning has been supported by history, the Holocaust, in which tens — even hundreds — of thousands of Jews, who were not halakhically so considered were sent to their deaths because the Nazis considered them Jews. The problem has been especially grave in the State of Israel where the children of mixed marriages (in which the wife is not Jewish), who speak Hebrew, are educated in the spirit of Jewish history, subscribe to Israel nationalism and serve in the army, feel discriminated against in that they are not considered Jews and are not registered as Jews in the identity cards which they are, by law, required to carry. In fact, what they are campaigning for is a secular definition of Jew, which is, understandably, vigorously opposed by the Rabbinate of Israel and the religious political parties.

According to *halakhah* a proselyte terminates all former family ties and is considered a newly born child. According to the letter of the law, the proselyte would be thus permitted to marry his former relatives; however, the sages prohibited it "so that they should not say: 'We have come from a greater sanctity to a lesser one.' " A male proselyte may marry a Jewish woman, even the daughter of a priest; however, a female proselyte may not marry a priest, unless her conversion took place before her third birthday.

A proselyte does not undergo the conventional mourning ceremonies after the death of his parents, and his former relatives do not inherit him. Thus, he begins his life as a Jew without kin, in a most difficult situation. It is for this reason that the Bible often reminds Jews to be exceptionally responsive to the needs of the proselyte, just as one would respond to the wishes of the widow and orphan, who are similarly without family.

4. BIRTH

I will continue to hold my banner aloft. I find myself born — ay, born — into a people and a religion. The preservation of my people must be for a purpose, for God does nothing without a purpose. His reasons are unfathomable to me, but on my own reason I place little dependence; test it where I will it fails me. The simple, the ultimate in every direction is sealed to me. It is as difficult to understand matter as mind. The courses of the planets are no harder to explain than the growth of a blade of grass. Therefore am I willing to remain a link in the great chain.

Cyrus Adler

Pregnancy

There is nothing in the universe more mystifying than the act of creation, and no act of creation more mystifying than the creation of the human being. Strangely, there is no information in the Bible about conception or birth. The Talmud, however, is intrigued by the subject and there are many discussions, often detailed, on the biological and theological aspects of conception and birth. Some of the facts are based on scientific knowledge, or on what the rabbis considered to be scientific knowledge, many are plainly folkloristic and many are homilies aimed at teaching the listeners the desired attitudes.

According to a talmudic homily, there are three partners in Partners in Man man: God, the father and the mother. The father supplies the white substance of which the child's bones, sinews, nails, brain and the white of the eyes are formed. The mother supplies the red substance of which are formed the skin, flesh, hair, blood, and the dark of the eyes. God supplies the spirit, the breath, beauty of features, eyesight, hearing, and the ability to speak and to walk, understanding and discernment. At death, God reclaims His part and leaves the father and mother with their part.

A detailed description of the fetus in the mother's womb is The Fetus also given in the Talmud: "Its hands rest on its two temples, its two elbows on its two legs and its two heels against its buttocks; its head lies between its knees; its mouth is closed and its navel is open, and it eats what its mother eats and drinks what its mother drinks, but produces no excrements because otherwise it might kill its mother; a light burns above its head and it is able to see from one end of the world to the other; it is taught all of the Torah, which the touch of an angel causes it to forget just before it is born." Folklore has it that the indentation on the upper lip is a sign of that touch. "There is no time a man spends on earth that he enjoys more than the time he spends in the womb. Before it is allowed to emerge, the child must take an oath to be righteous and never to be wicked; and although the whole world should someday proclaim it to be righteous, the child must still see itself as wicked in an effort at self-improvement. The child is also instructed to bear in mind that the Holy One is pure, that His creations are pure, and that the soul which it receives is pure. If the soul is preserved in purity, well and good, but if not, it will be taken away."

The Talmud divided the nine months of pregnancy into three Nine Months equal periods. In the first period the embryo occupies the lowest chamber of the womb, and sexual intercourse during this period is said to be "hard" for both mother and child. In the middle period the embryo occupies the middle chamber; intercourse is

"Maternity" by Meijer de Haan, 1890 (opposite).

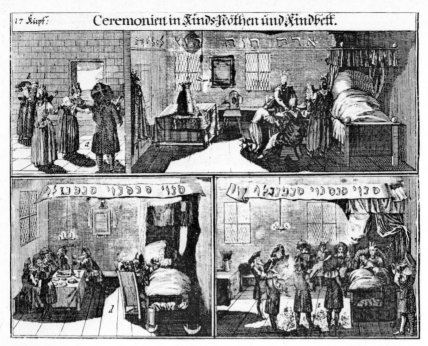

An 18th century copper engraving in three parts: on top a woman is assisted in childbirth as friends pray for her well-being outside the room. Note the Torah Scroll inside her chambers. After the birth, she is visited by friends and a sword is placed above her head for protection (bottom right). Finally, a festive meal to celebrate the occasion (bottom left).

then "hard" for the mother but good for the embryo. In the last period the embryo occupies the uppermost chamber and intercourse is beneficial both for mother and child as it aids in developing a well-formed child and gives it vitality. Rashi, the famous 11th century Talmud commentator remarks on this passage, "I do not know what 'hard' means."

The ninetieth day of pregnancy was considered to be a crucial point for the survival of the fetus. The scholars of the Talmud were in agreement that intercourse on the ninetieth day could easily cause injury to the fetus, leading one of them to

The Ninetiet
Day

36

Protective amulet for childbirth. The amulet guarded the mother prior to her giving birth and mother and child after the birth.

prohibit intercourse on that day. However, another rabbi, aware of the difficulty in calculating the date precisely, did not advise marital separation but summoned divine protection for the mother and child.

The miracle of childbirth was also used to contrast the capabilities of God and man. "What does Scripture teach by the verse 'Who doeth great things past finding out; yea, marvellous things without number?' Notice! A man puts things in a closed skin bottle with the opening facing upwards and yet the contents may or may not be preserved. God, on the other hand, places the embryo in an open womb with the orifice facing downwards and yet it is preserved." In addition, the rabbis ask, "What is taught by the verse, 'I will give thanks unto Thee, for I am fearfully and wonderfully made; Wonderful are Thy works; and that my soul knoweth right well'? Notice the difference between God and man! A man puts different seeds together in the soil and each grows in the manner of its own species; whereas God places the embryo in the mother's womb with the result that both the father's and mother's seed grow into one and the same species." Another parable was given: "Compare! The clothesdyer places

The Miracle

37

several dyes in the vat and yet all unite to form one color, whereas God places the embryo in the womb such that each element of the parent's seed develops in its own natural way."

The determination of the child's sex also interested the sages. Based on the biblical verse, "If a woman brings forth seed, and bears a man-child . . . ", they taught that, if during sexual intercourse the woman emits her seed (achieves her orgasm?) before the man, the child will be a boy. Otherwise, it will be a girl. Therefore, the Talmud suggests, if a man wants male offspring he should either hold back his own orgasm or cohabit twice in succession in which case it is assured that the wife will "bring forth seed" first.

Determinati of Sex

Folklore

Whereas much was written on pregnancy in the Talmud, there is very little material concerning the actual birth. Indeed, most of the customs — medieval and modern — surrounding birth belong to the category of popular folklore, much of which is not distinctively Jewish but has been adapted from local cultural surroundings. Some customs were introduced as sympathetic measures to ease the mental strains and sufferings of the woman. In order to ward off evil spirits, for example, a magic circle of chalk or charcoal used to be drawn on the floor of the room around her bed. To assure an easy and speedy delivery, all the knots and ties in the woman's garment were undone and all the doors of the house were opened wide. If the delivery proved difficult, the keys of the synagogue were placed in her hand, she was girded with the belt from around the Torah Scroll, and prayers were recited at the graveside of pious relatives. At times, the cemetery walls were measured and a number of candles making up their distance were donated to the synagogue or a procession went around the cemetery walls reciting Psalms and penitential prayers. Today too, prayers are often recited for the protection of women in labor.

Evil Spirits

Birth amulet listing the names of the Patriarchs and Matriarchs, with those of Adam and Eve, in the central column. Rachel, who died in childbirth, is not listed. The Hebrew and Aramaic text is an invocation against Lilith. Algeria, 20th century.

Amulets

In Oriental countries a particularly popular method of protecting the mother from evil spirits was the use of amulets in the shape of the palm of the hand and fingers, or resembling a seven-branched candelabrum. It was also customary to place sweet-meats under the mother's bed to appease the evil spirits who ate them and did not harm the mother and child. In Salonika the doors of the house and all the cupboards were left open during pregnancy to ensure that the mother would not miscarry. In some places it was customary to measure a string seven times around the grave of a renowned rabbi and then bind it around

39

the stomach of the pregnant woman to ensure an easy pregnancy. To ensure that the child would be a male, the mother pronounced the intended name of a boy every Friday.

After childbirth, both the mother and child were given similar protection. In Salonika the mother was to stay awake for three days after childbirth to protect her from Lilith, a female demon, who according to legend cannot herself bear children and so is jealous. In Kurdistan the mother was not allowed to leave the house after nightfall for forty days after giving birth.

> Amulet for childbirth to be hung in the delivery room, Amsterdam, 17th century, engraved by Abram bar Jacob. According to the legend, Lilith, the first wife of Adam, would harm the new born child. The text therefore reads, "out Lilith" and "Tear Satan into pieces."

Amulet for a mother who has given birth to her first son. The child was born on 5 Kislev 5594 (1833), Iraq.

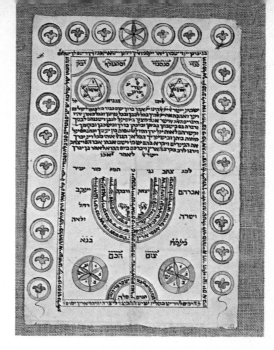

Chair of Elijah, Germany, 1768. This chair was kept in the synagogue. One seat was for the *sandak* while the other was reserved for the prophet Elijah. Over the seat the benefactor's name and year of donation are inscribed.

A *bar mitzvah* ceremony at the Western Wall. In the background is the reconstructed Jewish Quarter of the Old City.

A *bar mitzvah* ceremony in the synagogue of the Hadassah Medical Center in Jerusalem. The colorful stained glass windows in the background depicting the tribes of Israel were designed by Marc Chagall.

A male child particularly had to be protected from Lilith. In some places, mother and son were protected by various charms and talismans which were placed above the bed and above the doorposts until the circumcision. Another popular custom until modern times was the vigil ceremony which was performed every night until circumcision. Friends and relatives gathered nightly at the home of the newborn to recite biblical passages. School children, led by their teachers, also participated and were rewarded with apples, nuts, and sweets.

A universal weapon against demons is iron, and sometimes *Weapons* even a weapon of iron such as a sword or knife was placed under the bed of the mother and in the baby's cradle. According to folk belief, the circumcision knife had great protective powers if placed in the child's cradle on the night prior to the circumcision, that night being the most critical.

In Oriental countries similar methods were utilized to protect mother and infant from evil spirits. There were places where the child was guarded by blue beads, ivory or coral which were hung above its head. Garlic was hung around the room, and an open hand painted on the door. In Eastern Europe, the baby was protected by a red ribbon tied around its wrists.

Whereas a boy is named at the circumcision, a girl is usually *Naming the Child* named in the synagogue, when the father can be called to the reading of the Torah. Another custom was to name a girl when her mother visited the synagogue for the first time after childbirth. In Germany and Western Europe the naming took place in a ceremony at home on a Sabbath morning, while in Yemen the child was named at a festive meal on the third day after birth.

A ceremony still in practice today is the *sholem zokhor* *Sholem Zokhor* which means "peace (or welcome) to the male child." It is usually held on the first Friday evening after the birth of a boy, although in some communities it is held on the evening prior to circumcision. For the *sholem zokhor*, relatives and friends gather at the home of the child's parents in order to congratulate them.

41

After reciting biblical passages and Psalms, the guests are served drinks, cakes, and fruits; in some places also lentils and chickpeas. Lentils, due to their round shape, symbolize the ever-recurring life cycle. They are also served at a mourner's table to symbolize the continuity of life. At the *sholem zokhor,* which is a happy occasion, they are served as a consolation for the sadness felt because the child has forgotten all the Torah he learned in the mother's womb. In Oriental communities, the *sholem zokhor* is also known as *shasha* or *blada* and includes the recital of special prayers and aggadic readings in honor of the Prophet Elijah, the patron of the child at circumcision. Participation in the *sholem zokhor* is considered a *mitzvah.*

Rather similar to astrology is the talmudic belief that the time of birth will affect the character of the child. Based on the biblical story of the Creation, some sages taught that there was a direct connection between the days of the week and the characters of those born on those days: thus, a person born on Sunday will have one dominant attribute, either good or bad; a person born on Monday will be irascible; a Tuesday baby will be wealthy and unchaste; a Wednesday baby will be intelligent; a Thursday child will be benevolent; a person born on the Sabbath will be a great and holy man. However, according to another opinion in the Talmud, it was not the day, but rather the constellation that determined the character. Thus, "He who is born under the constellation of the sun will be a distinguished man: he will eat and drink of his own and his secrets will lie uncovered; if a thief, he will have no success. He who is born under Venus will be wealthy and unchaste . . . He who is born under Mercury will be of a retentive memory and wise . . . He who is born under the moon will be a man to suffer evil . . . if a thief, he will be successful. He who is born under Saturn will be a man whose plans will be frustrated . . . He who is born under Jupiter will be a right-doing man . . . He who is born under Mars will be a shedder of blood." The last mentioned was advised to become a ritual slaughterer *(shoḥet),* and thus fulfill his destiny in a legal manner.

Halakhah

Whereas most of childbirth is surrounded by folklore, one aspect, the sexual relations of the parents after birth, is dealt with extensively in the law codes. The basic law is stated in the Bible, and according to its literal meaning, a woman is prohibited from having intercourse for seven days following the birth of a male child, and for fourteen days if she gives birth to a girl. A further period of thirty three days in the former instance and sixty six days in the latter is laid down, these being the "days of her purification," during which any blood seen is "the blood of purification," when she is permitted to have relations with her

Torah wrapper made of white linen, lavishly embroidered with colored silk, Germany. The inscription is, "Ḥayyim son of Judah Gomperz born on the 18th day of Elul, 6573 (1813)." The figures include the zodiacal sign Virgo.

husband. After her period of purification has elapsed, she must bring prescribed sacrifices. The requirement to bring sacrifices was explained by the suggestion that under the stress of childbirth, the woman could well have vowed never to cohabit with her husband again, a vow she would not want to keep. For this sin she must bring a sacrifice (a practice not kept since the destruction of the Temple in Jerusalem in 70 c.e.). The law of sexual relations was preserved in this form by the sages, who added, however, that any blood seen during the "days of her purification" renders her prohibited to her husband and requires her, when the blood flow ceases, to immerse herself in the *mikveh* (ritual bath) at which time she becomes 'clean'. Later, it became the custom in Babylonia, Erez Israel, Spain, and North Africa that a woman after childbirth observed seven clean days for any blood seen during her "days of purification". This custom was not accepted in medieval France and Germany (where sexual intercourse was permitted even after a discharge during the days of purification), but it is today the generally accepted practice. A more stringent custom exists whereby sexual intercourse is prohibited during all of the forty days after a boy, and eighty days after a girl even though no blood whatsoever has been seen. This custom was regarded by Maimonides as "the way of heretics"; and is practiced by the Karaites and also by the Falashas.

Sacrifices

"Dedication to the Torah" by Moritz Oppenheim, 1869. The painting shows a father holding an infant near the Torah Scroll. On the Torah is a *wimpel*, a band of linen made from the child's circumcision diaper. The dedication ceremony was prevalent among German Jews and usually took place when the child was a year old (opposite).

To every thing there is a season, and a time to every
purpose under the heaven:
A time to be born, and a time to die;
A time to plant, and a time to pluck up that which is
planted;
A time to kill, and a time to heal;
A time to break down, and a time to build up;
A time to weep, and a time to laugh;
A time to mourn, and a time to dance.

Ecclesiastes

Birth Pains

In the biblical scheme of things childbirth was originally meant to be painless. However, as a punishment for Eve's disobedience in eating from the forbidden fruit of the Garden of Eden, the pains and perils of giving birth were ordained. Some of the prophets speak of the pain suffered in childbirth as the most severe to be experienced in life. The Bible records the deaths of Rachel and the daughter-in-law of Eli (the High Priest) in childbirth, and the Talmud adds that Michal, King David's wife, also died during childbirth. In the Mishnah, death in childbirth is attributed to a woman's neglect of those commandments specially applying to women: the laws of the menstruous woman *(niddah)*, failure to separate the tithe of dough from the bread she bakes *(hallah)*, and negligence in kindling the Sabbath lights *(hadlakat ha-ner)*.

Accidental Abortion

Judaism, which sees the preservation of life as one of the highest ideals, seeks due justification for interrupting nature's course, and deals with the problem of abortion. The Bible itself treats only accidental abortion. "And if men strive together, and hurt a woman with child, so that her fruit depart, and yet no

46

The birth of Benjamin, with Jacob standing by the dying Rachel.
From a Latin Bible, *Biblia Pauperum*, 15th century.

harm follow — he shall be surely freed . . . But if any harm follow
— then thou shall give life for life." The question is raised — to
whom does the term "harm" refer, mother or child? According
to the Septuagint (the oldest Greek translation of the Bible), the
term applies to the fetus and not the woman, and a distinction is
drawn between the abortion of a fetus which has not yet
assumed complete shape, for which there is a monetary penalty,
and the abortion of a fetus which is completely formed, for

47

which the penalty is "life for life." The talmudic scholars, however, maintained that the term "harm" refers to the mother and not the fetus. The word "man" in the scriptural injunction, "He that smiteth a man so that he dieth, shall surely be put to death", thus applies to a born person and not a fetus. In Jewish law, therefore, abortion, although prohibited, is not a punishable crime unless the victim is viable. Hence, even if an infant is only one day old, killing it constitutes murder. In the view of Rabbi Ishmael, only a gentile to whom some of the basic transgressions (murder, incest, idolatry, etc.) apply with greater stringency, incurs the death penalty for the destruction of a fetus. Thus, abortion, although prohibited, does not constitute murder. The prohibition was deduced from the prohibitive laws concerning abstention from procreation, or onanism, or having sexual relations with one's wife when this is likely to harm the fetus — the perpetrator whereof being regarded as "a shedder of blood". This is apparently also the meaning of Josephus' statement that "the law has commanded to raise all the children and prohibited women from aborting or destroying seed; a woman who does so shall be judged a murderess of children for she has caused a soul to be lost and the family of man to be diminished."

Abortion is definitely permitted in Jewish law if the fetus *Danger to* endangers the mother's life. Thus, "if a woman is in labor (and it *Mother's L* is feared she may die), one may sever the fetus from her womb and extract it, member by member, for her life takes precedence over his." This is the case only as long as the fetus has not emerged into the world, and is thus not yet viable — "it may be killed and the mother saved." However, once either the head or the greater part of the child's body emerges into the world, it is considered to be viable and, as such, has the same right to life as the mother, and killing it is no longer permitted.

The law states that one must do everything in one's power to *Law of Purs* rescue a person who is being pursued by another with intent to kill, even to the extent of killing the pursuer. This does not apply to a fetus, however, which has emerged into the world since "she (the mother) is pursued from heaven," and not by man, and moreover, "such (difficulty in childbirth) is the way of the world," and "one does not know whether the fetus is pursuing the mother or the mother the fetus." However, when the mother's life is endangered, she herself may destroy the fetus, even if its greater part of head has emerged, "for even if, in the eyes of others, the law of a fetus is not as the law of the pursuer, the mother may yet regard it as pursuing her."

Is, however, abortion permitted when the fetus has not emerged but is not endangering the mother's life? Some authorities prohibit abortion in this case; they derive their proof from the statement "because it is pursuing to kill her," thereby prohibiting abortion except when the mother's illness is a result of the pregnancy. The majority of later authorities, however, maintain that abortion should be permitted if it is necessary for the general welfare of the mother, even if there is no mortal danger to her because of pregnancy, and even if the mother's illness has not been directly caused by the fetus. Rabbi Jacob Emden (1697–1776) permitted abortion "as long as the fetus has not emerged from the womb, even if not in order to save the mother's life, but only to save her from the harassment and great pain which the fetus causes her." A similar view was adopted by Benzion Meir Hai Uziel, the late Sephardi Chief Rabbi of Israel; namely that abortion is prohibited if merely intended for its own sake, but permitted "if intended to serve the mother's needs, even if not vital." He accordingly ruled, for example, that abortion was permissible to save the mother from deafness which would result, according to medical opinion, from her continued pregnancy. In the Kovno ghetto, during the Holocaust, the Nazis decreed that any Jewish woman who became pregnant would be executed and Rabbi Ephraim Oshey ruled that an abortion was permissible in order to save a pregnant woman from the consequences of the inhuman law.

49

The permissibility of an abortion has also been discussed in relation to a pregnancy resulting from a prohibited (i.e., adulterous or incestuous) union. Rabbi Jacob Emden permitted an abortion to a married woman pregnant by adultery, since the child would be a *mamzer,* but not to an unmarried woman, since the taint of bastardy does not attach to her offspring. In a later responsum it was decided that abortion was prohibited even in the former case, but this decision was reversed by Rabbi Uziel, in deciding that in the case of bastardy abortion was permissible at the hands of the mother herself. *Prohibited Unions*

In recent years the question of permissibility of an abortion has been raised in cases where there is reason to expect that the child will suffer from a mental or physical defect because of an illness, such as rubella or measles, contracted by the mother or due to the effects of drugs, such as thalidomide. The general tendency is to uphold the prohibition against abortion in such cases, unless justified in the interests of the mother's health. This factor has, however, been deemed to extend to profound *Suffering of Child*

50

A *Kimpetbriefl,* protective amulet for women in childbirth. In the center is Psalm 121 surrounded by the names of the Patriarchs and Matriarchs (except Rachel), Hungary, 1883.

emotional or mental disturbance. An important factor in deciding whether or not an abortion should be permitted is the stage of the pregnancy: the earlier the problem is raised, the stronger the considerations in favor of permitting an abortion.

In general, it may be said that the cautious veiw Judaism takes of abortion reflects its attitude to life as a gift granted by God, which is not to be taken lightly.

6. CIRCUMCISION

Israel, my people
God's greatest riddle,
Will thy solution
Ever be told?

P. M. Raskin

Of all the rites and ceremonies in Jewish life, it is in the rite of circumcision that the familial aspect of the *mitzvot* comes most clearly to the fore. In the course of this ceremony, it is the father who is obligated with the fulfillment of the precept; grand-parents, uncles and aunts are commonly honored with participation in the ritual; and the prayers recited both at the ceremony and in the grace after the festive meal — itself a family occasion par excellence — invoke divine assistance to the parents in their task of bringing up their child.

History

Although according to rabbinic tradition circumcision was *In the Bible* known before the time of Abraham, it was among the Hebrews that it became firmly established. The Bible relates that Abraham circumcised himself at the age of ninety nine in compliance with

"The Child Entering the Covenant," an oil painting by M. Oppenheim, Germany, 1837. The baby is brought to the synagogue and handed over at the door to an honored guest. The *sandak* and *mohel* await the baby's arrival.

the commandment, "Every male among you shall be circumcised. And ye shall be circumcised in the flesh of your foreskin, and it shall be a token of a covenant betwixt Me and you. And he that is eight days old shall be circumcised among you, every male throughout your generations." Abraham also circumcised his son Ishmael and all the males of his household. In the following year, when Isaac was born, he was circumcised on the eighth day. When Jacob's daughter Dinah was seduced by the Hivite prince Shechem and the question of their marriage arose, the sons of Jacob insisted that the Hivites undergo the rite. Several generations later, when Moses neglected to circumcise his own son, the fault was repaired by his wife Zipporah. Before the Israelites entered Canaan, they were circumcised by Joshua, the rite having being omitted for their forty years of wandering in the wilderness owing to the hazards of the journey.

The circumcision ceremony. A woodcut from the Amsterdam *Minhagim Book*, 1661.

The importance that the Bible attaches to circumcision is evident from the repeated contemptuous references to the Philistines as being uncircumcised, a factor that gave the Israelites power over them. However, there was a period in the Kingdom of Israel under the influence of Queen Jezebel, when circumcision was abandoned. Elijah's zeal in persuading the Israelites to resume the forsaken covenant won him the name "Herald of the Covenant" and his memory plays an important part in today's ritual. The prophet Ezekiel is full of contempt for the uncircumcised heathen whose fate he fortells. In Hellenistic times (4th–2nd centuries b.c.e.), according to the Book of Jubilees, circumcision was widely neglected. Many Jews who had undergone circumcision and wanted to participate nude in the Greek games in the gymnasia underwent painful surgery to obliterate the signs of circumcision to the derision and scorn of those whom they were trying to imitate. According to the Midrash, when David looked upon himself naked in the bath chamber, he was distressed that he bore no religious insignia such as *tefillin* until he noticed the circumcision, whereupon in praise of the Almighty, he composed Psalm 12.

In the second century b.c.e. the first definite prohibition against circumcision was enacted by Antiochus Epiphanes. Many mothers had their sons circumcised and suffered martyrdom for it. It is recorded that two women who had circumcised their children were led round the walls of their city with their babes bound to their breasts and then cast headlong from the wall. With the victory of the Hasmoneans (162 b.c.e.) and the extension of the frontiers of Israel, King John Hyrcanus forced the conquered Idumeans to undergo circumcision. Religious leaders at the time, however, differed about the necessity of circumcision for acceptance of proselytes (see page 31). The custom of circumcision seems to have spread among the Romans in the Diaspora under the influence of the Jewish community in Rome. When a Roman official asked Rabbi Oshaya why God had not

Circumcision pillow. The baby is placed on the pillow and held in position by the *sandak*. The center illustration shows Elijah and the city of Jerusalem.

made man as He wanted him, he replied that it was in order that man should perfect himself by the fulfillment of a divine command. However, the Roman Emperor Hadrian (117–138) proscribed circumcision for the Jews, and this was one of the causes of the Bar Kokhba rebellion. With the rise of Christianity, circumcision became the difference between the adherents of the two religions since Paul declared that justification by faith was sufficient for converts to Christianity. In Justinian's *Codex* (535 c.e.) surgeons were prohibited from performing the operation on Roman citizens who converted to Judaism.

Circumcision has been one of the most constantly observed rituals of the Jew, although at times, it was difficult to perform. In some periods as in the present, the operation was generally widespread because of the approval of medical science. Circumcision in Judaism, however, is not only a medical operation; it is an important *mitzvah* and thus a part of the law code.

Halakhah

It is the duty of every Jewish father to have his son circumcised. Should he neglect to do so, it devolves on the *bet din* (court of law). It is not, however, a sacrament and any child born to a Jewish mother is a Jew, whether circumcised or not. Although circumcision may be performed by any Jew (or Jewess, if no male is available), it is most desirable that the operator, called a *mohel*, be a pious observant Jew. As early as in talmudic times, the *mohel* was described as a craftsman, and in most modern communities, he has been specially trained in the principles of asepsis and in the techniques of circumcision as well as having received rabbinic recognition.

"The Circumcision," oil painting by Rembrandt. Note that the mother is holding the child, while the rabbi recites prayers.

"The Daughter Introduces Her Fiancé," by Moritz Daniel Oppenheim, 1860.

אשת חיל
עטרת בעלה

סדר של שלש מצ'ות
להנשים ❖ חלה ❖ נדה ❖
הדלקה ❖ סימן חנה ❖

נעבט די זאה קין לכרבן חין הנגרן סלייבט ועלבט
ין נוהג נין דרהו בנין ❖ ועשט מיר חבר רעבכטטוהן
כר בדעונט די חלה זעובר ❖

הריני מוכן ומזומן לקיים
המצוה עשה ❖ לשם יקבה

ושכינתיה על ידי ההוא אנטמיר ונעלם ב ב ל

A 19th century copy of a majolica Sabbath plate by Isaac Azulai, Faenza, 1575. Central text reads *Eshet ḥayil . . . ateret ba'alah,* "A woman of valor is her husband's crown".

Page from a woman's ritual manual, showing two women making *ḥallah* (loaves) for Shabbat. Austria (?), 1751.

The Ceremony

The operation should be performed on the eighth day after birth, *Time* preferably early in the morning, thus emulating Abraham in his eagerness to obey the divine command. Should the child be premature or in poor health, the rite must be postponed until seven days after he has recovered from a general disease or until immediately after recovery from a local disorder. Should a child for any reason have been circumcised before the eighth day or have been born already circumcised (i.e., without a foreskin), the ceremony of "drawing the blood of the covenant" must be performed on the eighth day, provided it is a weekday and the child is fit. This is done by puncturing the skin of the glans with a scalpel or needle and allowing a drop of blood to exude.

The performance of the commandment on the eighth day *The Sabbath and Festivals* after birth takes precedence over the laws normally governing the sanctity of the Sabbath and festivals. Preparations for the operation, such as bringing the utensils to the place of circumcision, should be completed before the Sabbath. The Sabbath and festival laws, however, are not set aside in certain exceptional cases, such as the above mentioned case of the "drawing of the blood of the covenant," the case of a child born by Caesarian section, or in the case of a child born during twilight of the Sabbath or a festival (because the precise dating of his birth is open to question).

The ritual begins when the child is brought from the mother *Presenting the Child* by the godmother, and handed over at the door of the room to the godfather who, in turn, hands it to the *mohel*. Before this, the child is welcomed by the congregation with *Barukh ha-ba* ("Blessed be he that comes"). The Sephardim sing a special hymn in which praise is given to those who keep the covenant. The *mohel* places the baby for a moment on the chair of Elijah, *Chair of Elijah* which is a special, ornate chair left unoccupied. The chair is meant for the prophet Elijah who in spirit attends all circumcisions as it was he who accused Israel of not performing the

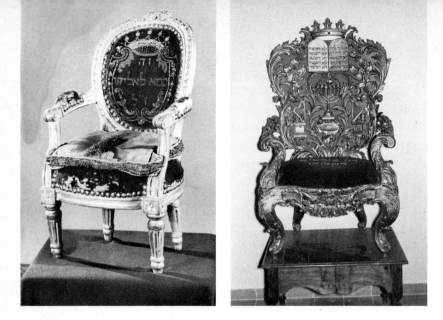

Chair of Elijah from Carpentras (left) and Rome (right). The chair remains empty throughout the ceremony except for a brief moment when the baby is placed in it and the *mohel* says, "This is the Chair of Elijah the Prophet, may he be remembered for good."

ritual of the covenant, and God is said to have told Elijah: "Because of the excessive zeal for Me, you have brought charges against Israel that they have forsaken My covenant; therefore ye shall have to be present at every circumcision ceremony." His presence is also desired, Elijah being the guardian angel of children; perhaps the biblical story in which he revived the child of the widow created this image. When the *mohel* places the child in Elijah's chair he says, "This is the chair of Elijah, blessed be his memory," and then picks the child up and places him on a pillow in the lap of the *sandak* ("holder"; godfather) who is sitting in a chair adjacent to that of Elijah's. The infant's legs are held firmly by the *sandak;* the *mohel,* having previously thoroughly scrubbed and immersed his hands in a disinfectant solution, takes a firm

The Sandak

58

grip of the foreskin with his left hand. He determines the amount to be removed and fixes a shield on it to protect the glans from injury. The knife, sometimes double-edged, is then taken in the right hand and, after the recitation of the benediction, "Who has commanded us on circumcision", the foreskin is amputated with one sweep along the shield. This discloses the mucous membrane, the edge of which is then grasped firmly between the thumbnail and index finger of each hand and is torn down the center as far as the corona. This part of the operation is called *periah*. Sometimes this maneuver is performed with scissors, but it is known that a lacerated wound is much less likely to bleed than a cut wound. *The Knife* *Periah*

Since the middle of the nineteenth century, when Dr. Terquem of Metz published his *Guide for Circumcision* (including a new procedure to deal with *periah*), a large number of new instruments have been devised for the performance of the operation. The latest in the series have been the clamp and, more recently, the bell. However, none of these methods excels the traditional Jewish practice, described above, for speed and minimal trauma to the infant.

The next stage is the performance of *meẓiẓah* ("suction") which has led to much controversy in recent years. Throughout the ages this was done orally which according to Maimonides removed the blood from the distant parts of the wound. This was the recognized method of healing at the time. A *mohel* who did not perform it was considered to be endangering the life of the child, and was debarred from practice. Toward the middle of the nineteenth and beginning of the twentieth centuries, cases of syphilis, tuberculosis, and diptheria occurring in infants were ascribed to infection from *mohalim* using this method of suction. This has been contested by some Jewish doctors, and in some communities the original practice is still followed. The Paris Consistoire abolished oral *meẓiẓah* in 1843. The method now authorized by most rabbinical courts is for *meẓiẓah* to be per- *Meẓiẓah*

59

Circumcision equipment. On top is prayerbook with instructions for carrying out the ceremony, by Jacob Sofer ben Judah Loeb of Berlin, 1729. In front is a bowl for foreskin (Germany, 18th century), a bottle for wine or disinfectants (Italy, 18th/19th century), a knife (Near East, 1819), and a shield used to guide the *mohel* in the incision (France,19th century).

formed either by a swab or through a glass tube, preferably containing a small piece of absorbent cotton. The rounded end of the tube is placed firmly over the penis, pressed firmly over the area of the pubis, and suction by the mouth is carried out through the flattened end of the tube or through a rubber attachment. This is followed by the application of a sterile dressing, and the replacing of the baby's diaper.

Immediately after the actual circumcision, the father recites the benediction, "Blessed art Thou, O Lord our God, Who hast hallowed us by Thy commandments and has commanded us to bring our sons into the covenant of Abraham our patriarch." In Israel, following the opinion of Rabbi Joseph Caro (1488–1575) the *she-heḥeyanu* benediction is recited. Outside Israel it is not customary to recite this benediction, in compliance with the opinion of Rabbi Moses Isserles (1525–1572) that pronouncing such a joyous benediction is out of place in a ceremony which involves pain to the child. Following the father's benediction, the guests proclaim, "Just as this child has entered into the covenant (of circumcision), so may he enter the (world of) Torah, the nuptial canopy, and good deeds." *Benedictions*

The sages took an active interest in the incidence of hemorrhage after the operation. According to modern scholars, hemophilia was recognized in talmudic times as a disease suffered by men but carried only by women, because the law is that a mother who has lost two children because of circumcision must not have her subsequent sons circumcised until they are older and better able to undergo the operation. Moreover, should two sisters each have lost a son from the effects of circumcision, the other sisters must not have their sons circumcised. *Medical Care*

The child is then handed to the father or to an honored guest, and the *mohel,* holding a goblet of wine, recites the benediction for wine and a second benediction praising God for His covenant with Israel. The *mohel* then makes an invocation for the welfare of the child during which the child is named. It is

61

Engraved pewter *mohel's* box, Bohemia, 17th/18th centuries. The box, in the shape of a child's crib, was used as a container for the *mohel's* equipment.

customary for the *mohel* to give the infant a few drops of wine to drink. The ceremony is followed by a festive meal at which special hymns are sung, and in the Grace after Meals, blessings are recited for the child, the parents, the *sandak*, and the *mohel.*

In the Middle Ages the ceremony was frequently performed in the synagogue, and still is today in some communities. There are set parts of the synagogue service during which it should take place. For the most part, however, the ceremony nowadays takes place in the hospital or at home; in Israel, maternity clinics have large rooms, where the ceremony and festivities take place.

In Jewish Thought

Philo was the first Jewish writer to advance hygienic reasons for circumcision, but these have never been used to justify it in the Jewish religion. When performed in infancy, it appears to be a complete protection against subsequent development of cancer of the penis, probably caused by the retention of smegma, a secretion of the mucous membrane of the foreskin. This factor is also considered by some authorities to be a cause of cancer of the cervix in women. Circumcision also protects against inflammation of the prepuce and glans. At the beginning of the twentieth century, it was the practice to treat bed-wetting, masturbation, and many children's disorders by circumcision, with negative results. This led to a tendency in some countries to avoid the operation altogether: In North America and Australia where the climate fluctuates to both extreme cold and heat, the latter disposing to inflammation of the prepuce, the practice is to circumcise in early infancy.

Although, as mentioned above, a male child born of a Jewish mother is a Jew whether or not circumcised, an uncircumcised Jew may not partake of the paschal lamb, and according to Ezekiel he will be doomed to enter *Gehenna* (hell). On the other hand, the circumcised, by that very virtue, merit entry into heaven. According to the Midrash, Abraham himself sits at the gates of hell to save the circumcised and God tells him that the continued existence of the world depends solely on the continued performance of the single precept of circumcision. Similarly, the abandonment of the circumcision ritual is implied, according to the Talmud, in the verse in Jeremiah: "Thus saith the Lord: If My covenant be not day and night, I would not have fixed the ordinances of heaven and earth."

In addition, the circumcised merit God's protection. *Protection* Josephus relates that when Queen Helena and her son, Izates, accepted Judaism, the latter's conversion aroused much opposition, and his opponents sought and received military assistance from Arabia to depose him. After several setbacks, Izates succeeded in routing the enemy. This miraculous victory is attributed to his having kept the covenant of circumcision.

The circumcision scene by Bernard Picart, Holland, 1722.

Reform Judaism, while not completely abolishing circum- *Reform Jud* cision, has emphasized the law that a Jew is a person born of a Jewish mother, whether he be circumcised or not. It is preferable to have a child circumcised in infancy, when there is little or no pain, and an older person who has not undergone circumcision

64

should be persuaded to do so. The circumcision may be performed by anyone, including gentiles, although it is preferable to have a Jewish physician. It is, similarly, preferable to perform the ceremony on the eighth day, although a circumcision performed earlier is not objected to. In general, Reform practice relaxes the strictness of the Orthodox approach, however, the observance of the ceremony is continued.

It can be said that all movements in Judaism see the importance and significance of circumcision. Even Baruch Spinoza, the semi-apostate philosopher who was excommunicated said: "Such great importance do I attach to the sign of the covenant, that I am persuaded it is sufficient by itself to maintain the separate existence of the nation forever." *Spinoza*

7. FIRSTBORN

Our God and God of our fathers, preserve this child to his father and to his mother . . . Let the father rejoice in his offspring, and the mother be glad with the fruit of her body . . . This little child, may he become great. Even as he has entered into the covenant, so may he enter into the Torah, the nuptial canopy, and into good deeds.

Prayer Book

Status
The firstborn child has a special significance to most expectant parents. Its arrival is anticipated with excitement and many preparations are made which, for subsequent children, become routine and somewhat less special. If the firstborn child is a son, besides the economic benefits to the parents, his birth ensures a continuance of the family name. This is so even today when there is greater equality between the sexes.

65

The Redemption ceremony by Bernard Picart, Holland,
1722. The family is gathered around while the father
transacts his deal with the *kohen*.

In the Bible the firstborn male child has a special status with
respect to inheritance rights and certain religious regulations. The
firstborn gets two portions of his father's estate, as opposed to
one portion each for all the other brothers. This is given to him
because he is "the first fruit of his (father's) vigor," i.e., the
father's first child. The latter (cultic) birthright stems from the
concept that God has a claim on the first offspring who were to

*Father's
Firstborn*

*Mother's
Firstborn*

be devoted to Him as priests in the Tabernacle and Temple, but who, possibly because of their transgression of worshipping the Golden Calf in the desert, were replaced by the Levites.

In Religion
The firstborn's religious status derives from his being "the first issue of the (mother's) womb", i.e., the mother's first child. Thus, a man with several wives can be a father to several cultic firstborns, each wife giving birth to a firstborn son, but only *his* firstborn son receives inheritance privileges. On the other hand, a woman who remarries several times can give birth to only one cultic primogenitary, but may foster many sons with the unique inheritance privilege, each husband being the father of a firstborn son by her.

Although, as has been noted, firstborns have been replaced by the Levites, and except for a requirement to fast on the eve of Passover, no peculiar responsibility is relegated to them, it is still a biblical requirement for a father to redeem the cultic firstborn by a payment of five silver *shekels* to any *kohen* (priest) of his choice. Nowadays five United States silver dollars are considered to be the equivalent and there are even specially minted coins for this purpose. The obligation to redeem the firstborn son falls on the father and not the mother, and a *bet din* may force an unwilling father to comply with the command. If, however, a child who requires redemption is not redeemed by the time of his *bar mitzvah* (see page 103), he is obliged to redeem himself.

The Redemption Ceremony
The redemption takes place at a special ceremony known as *Time* *pidyon ha-ben* (literally, redemption of the son) which is held in the presence of the *kohen* and invited guests, and takes place on the thirty-first day after the birth. The thirty-first day is chosen because the child is not considered as fully viable for the purposes of redemption until he survives the first thirty days of

his life. Even if the child has not as yet been circumcised (e.g., for health reasons), the redemption still takes place. Only if the thirty-first day is a Sabbath or festival (or according to some scholars an intermediate festival day) when a money transaction is prohibited, is the ceremony postponed to the evening or the

Bowl, 17th century, used in the Redemption of the First-born ceremony. The baby is placed on a pillow inside the bowl and passed from *kohen* to father during the ceremony.

following day. During the ceremony the father presents his son, often on a specially embellished tray, to the *kohen*, who asks him, in an ancient Aramaic formula, whether he wishes to redeem his child or to leave the child with the *kohen*. In some sources the formula is given in Hebrew. The father, in reply, expressed the desire to keep his son, hands the redemption money to the *kohen*, and recites one benediction for the fulfillment of the commandment of redemption, and another benediction of thanksgiving. The *kohen*, three times pronouncing, "Your son is redeemed," returns the child to the father. This dialogue is purely symbolic; a declaration by the father that he prefers the money to the child has no legal validity. Finally, the *kohen* recites a benediction over a goblet of wine, invokes the priestly blessing on the child, and joins the invited guests at a festive banquet.

Firstborn redemption coins. Above, coins minted in honor of the liberation of Jerusalem in 1967, designed by Vivian Cohen, and below, coins minted by the Israel Government Coins and Medals Corporation, 1971.

Halakhah

Priests and Levites

Kohanim and *levites* need not redeem their firstborn. However, the firstborn son of a marriage between a *kohen* and a woman forbidden to him (e.g., a divorcée) does not have priestly rank and thus must be redeemed, although the father may, in this case, keep the redemption money himself. A son born of a woman who previously miscarried a fetus of more than forty days, does not need to be redeemed since he does not fulfill the requirement of being the first issue of the womb. Israelites, i.e., those not of priestly descent, whose wives are the daughters of *kohanim* or *levites* need not redeem their firstborn, but the son of a *kohen's* daughter and a non-Jew must be redeemed because his mother has forfeited her status and is no longer privileged with priestly rank. The firstborn son of a *levite's* daughter born under the same circumstances does not need to be redeemed because her relations with a non-Jew do not infringe on her status.

Doubtful Primogenitur

If there is a doubt concerning the primogeniture of a child, the child need not be redeemed, because of the rule, "He who wishes to exact money from his neighbor must prove that the debt exists," and here the *kohen* who is claiming that the child needs redemption, must bring proof of his case, which he cannot do. Up to modern times, if the child was an orphan, a small medallion bearing an inscription as to his status of being a firstborn was hung around his neck until such time as he redeemed himself. In more recent times it has become the custom for either the rabbinical court or one of the child's relatives to redeem him.

Fast of the Firstborn

The only specific religious observance required of the firstborn is his obligation to fast on the eve of Passover, a custom commemorating the miraculous deliverance of the firstborn Israelites in Egypt when all the Egyptian firstborns perished. All males whether firstborn to their father or only to their mother, and, in some opinions, even female firstborns are required to fast. If a child is too young to fast, his father fasts instead of him; if the father is a firstborn, the child's mother fasts in lieu of the child. However, since one is permitted to break this fast in order to participate in a meal accompanying a religious celebration (e.g., circumcision banquet) it became the custom to complete a tractate of Talmud on the morning of the eve of Passover and to accompany the completion with a festive meal at which all the firstborns participate. Having eaten, the firstborn is no longer required to complete the day's fast.

Inheritance Rights

The inheritance privilege of the firstborn depends solely on the biological relationship; even if such a son if born of a prohibited union, e.g., the son of a *kohen* and a divorcée, he is entitled to the benefit of his status. The prerogative of the firstborn never extends to a daughter, not even in a case where she is entitled to inheritance, i.e., when all the children are female, they divide the inheritance equally. A son born to a proselyte to Judaism who had sons before his conversion does not enjoy the prerogative of a firstborn since he is not "the first fruit of his (father's) vigor"; on the other hand, if an Israelite had a son by a non-Jewish woman and thereafter has a son by a Jewish woman, the latter son does enjoy the prerogative, since the former son is called her (the gentile's) and not his, son. A first son who is born after his father's death (i.e., in the case of twins) is not entitled to the

Detail from the *Golden Haggadah* showing the tenth plague of Egypt in which all the first-born Egyptians perished and the firstborn Jews were spared.

71

double inheritance since it is written, "he (the father) must acknowledge" and the father is no longer alive to do so. The father, however, by the fact that "he must acknowledge" cannot deny the firstborn his right to a double portion. This is clearly stated in the Bible in the case where a man has two wives, one whom he loves and the other whom he hates. Should the latter give birth first and that child be male, the father must recognize the child's inheritance rights even if the beloved wife gives birth to a male child as well.

8. ADOPTION

When trouble comes upon the congregation, it is not right for a man to say, 'I will eat and drink, and things will be peaceful for me'. Moses, our Teacher, always bore his share in the troubles of the congregation, as it is written, 'They took a stone and put it under him'. Could they not have given him a chair or a cushion? But then he said, 'Since the Israelites are in trouble, lo, I will bear my part with them, for he who bears his portion of the burden will live to enjoy the hour of consolation'. Woe to one who thinks, 'Ah, well, I will neglect my duty. Who can know whether I bear my part or not? ' Even the stones of the house, ay, the limbs of the trees shall testify against him, as it is written, 'For the stones will cry from the wall, and the limbs of the trees will testify'.

Talmud

In the Bible
Adopting a child and providing for his wellbeing are considered among the greatest acts of *ẓedakah* (justice — charity) which a Jew can perform. There are several stories in the Bible which,

72

Jerusalem family of Persian origin
gathered for the traditional Passover
seder in the grandfather's home.

Circumcision papercut designed to be placed near the
Chair of Elijah. It includes inscriptions pertaining to the
circumcision ceremony, and the prayers to be recited by
the *mohel*. It was given to the Synagogue of Fillehene
near Posen, Poland, 1841.

according to some scholars, are examples of adoption or perhaps forerunners to what is nowadays known as adoption. However, the Bible does not lable these cases as such, and many scholars argue that adoption was not practiced in that period.

Among the suggested sources for adoption in the Bible, the *Abraham* following are outstanding. Abraham, being childless, complained to God that Eliezer, his servant, would be his heir. Since in the ancient Near East only relatives, normally sons, could inherit, Abraham had probably adopted, or contemplated adopting, Eliezer. This passage is illuminated by the non-Hebrew practice in the ancient Near East of childless couples adopting a son, who would serve them in their lifetime and bury them and mourn them when they died, in return for which he would be designated their heir. If a natural child was subsequently born to the couple, he would be their chief heir and the adopted son would be second to him.

Jacob, near the end of his life, recalling God's promise of *Jacob* preserving the land of Canaan for his descendants, announced to Joseph: "Your two sons who were born to you . . . before I came to you in Egypt, shall be mine; Ephraim and Manasseh shall be mine, as Reuben and Simeon are." It is questionable whether Jacob meant to adopt Ephraim and Manasseh completely or merely to give them special inheritance rights. It must be remembered that the principals, Ephraim and Manasseh are grandsons of Jacob and not outsiders. Whether or not adoption was intended can be argued equally impressively from both sides.

During the slavery of the Israelites in Egypt, Pharaoh, fearful *Moses* of an Israelite rebellion, ordered all sons born to Jewesses to be cast into the Nile. Israelite women were careful to hide signs of their pregnancy and, when possible, deceive the authorities as to when they had given birth. One such woman Jochebed, gave birth in her sixth month, enabling her to hide the child for several months. When she could no longer continue this deception, she placed the child, later to be named Moses, in a basket among the

73

"Jacob Blessing the Sons of Joseph," an oil by Rembrandt, 1656.

reeds of the Nile. The child was found by Pharaoh's daughter, who provided for him and brought him up in the royal court. Scripture tells us: "Moses became her (Pharaoh's daughter's) son." Those who do not accept adoption as a Hebrew practice in biblical times regard the passage as a reflection of the Egyptian practice of adoption. Others explain the word "became" as referring to fosterage, i.e., support without legal ties, rather than true adoption.

74

"The Finding of Moses" by Veronese Paolo, Venice, c. 1570.
Pharaoh's daughter is seen looking at the infant Moses.

Perhaps the best proof for the existence of adoption in the *Mordecai*
Bible is the case of Mordecai's adoption of his niece Esther:
"And he (Mordecai) brought up Hadassah, that is, Esther, his
uncle's daughter; . . . and when her father and mother were dead,
Mordecai took her for his own daughter." This, however, may
only reflect a singular occurrence of Jews under Persian rule. The
Elephantine Jews of the fifth century under Persian rule were
known to have practiced adoption.

In addition to these cases, one may see a sort of posthumous *Levirate Mar*
adoption in the ascription of the firstborn of a levirate marriage
(marriage to the brother of a deceased husband) to the dead
brother. The child is called "A son of B (the deceased)". In this
way he preserves the deceased's name and presumably inherits his
property.

Thus there is a possibility that adoption was practiced in the
Bible. Nevertheless it seems that its importance in the Israelite
family was insignificant, for until very recently no Hebrew term
for adoption even existed.

Attitudes

Even so, great emphasis was placed on the treatment of orphans. *Maimonides*
Maimonides considered the good treatment of orphans as an
important aspect of every Jew's duty to be charitable. He wrote:

> "A man ought to be especially heedful of his behavior toward
> widows and orphans, for their souls are exceedingly
> depressed and their spirits low. Even if they are wealthy, even
> if they are the widow and orphans of a king, we are especially
> enjoined concerning them, as it is said, 'Ye shall not afflict
> any widow or orphan'. How are we to conduct ourselves
> toward them? One may not speak to them other than
> tenderly. One must show them unvarying courtesy; one must
> not hurt them physically with hard toil, nor wound their
> feelings with hard speech. One must take greater care of their
> property than of one's own. Whoever irritates them, provokes

them to anger, pains them, tyrannizes over them or causes them loss of money, is guilty of a transgression, and all the more so if one beats them. Though lashes are not inflicted for this transgression, its punishment is explicitly set forth in the Torah, 'My wrath shall wax hot, and I will slay you with the sword'. He Who created the world by His word made a covenant with widows and orphans that, when they cry out because of violence, they are answered; as it is written, 'If thou afflict them in any wise — for if they cry at all unto Me, I will surely hear their cry! ' The above only applies to cases where a person afflicts them for his own ends. But it is permissible for a teacher to punish orphan children in order to teach them Torah or a trade, or to lead them in the right way. And yet he should not treat them like the other children, but make a distinction in their favor. He should guide them gently, with the utmost tenderness and courtesy, as it is said, 'For the Lord will plead their cause'."

Although God is considered to be the sole protector of orphans: "A *Charity* father to the fatherless . . . is God in His holy habitation", talmudic scholars considered it an act of great charity to house and protect the orphan. "Happy are they that keep justice, that do righteousness at all times'. Is it possible to do righteousness at all times? . . . (Yes!) It refers to a man who brings up an orphan boy or girl in his home and enables him to marry," an act of unceasing charity.

In Law

However it may seem from the biblical sources, adoption as a *Biological* separate legal institution is unknown in talmudic law. According *Relationship* to the *halakhah,* the legal status of parent and child is dependent on the natural biological relationship only and there is no recognized way of creating this status artificially. Jewish law, however, does provide for consequences essentially similar to those caused by adoption to be created by legal means.

Jewish family from
Fez, Morocco, c. 1925.

These consequences are the right and obligation of a person *Guardian*
to assume responsibility for a child's physical and mental welfare
as well as his financial position, including inheritance and main-
tenance. This may be done by a court appointment of a
"guardian." The court is considered to be the "father of all
orphans", and as such it may delegate its authority.

The power of the court is not restricted to orphans. It may
appoint a guardian to serve together with the minor's father if, in
the opinion of the court, the latter is incapable of fully dis-

78

charging his duties towards the child. Furthermore, because the court is empowered to act in the best interest of the child, it may even, after proper consideration, order the removal of a minor from his parent's house and appoint a guardian over his person and property. Similarly, the court may terminate the appointment of the guardian.

The functions of a guardian are generally defined upon appointment, because guardianship in itself does not imply that the relationship will be as is that of a natural parent and child. Responsibility for the child can also be divided among several guardians. A guardian entrusted with the child's welfare will be responsible for the minor's upbringing, education, and determination of place of residence. The administration of the child's property is a separate responsibility which, in normal adoptive procedures, is entrusted to the same person, the adopting parent. On the death of the adopter, his heirs are obliged to continue to maintain the adopted child out of the former's estate. In principle, neither the rights of the child in respect to his natural parents, nor their obligations towards him are in any way affected by adoption. The primary question as to the extent the natural parents are to be deprived of, and the adoptive parents vested with the rights and obligations to look after the child's welfare, is decided in accordance with the rule that in all matters the overriding consideration is the child's welfare and interests. *Functions of the Guardian*

From the legal point of view, an adopted child simply acquires an additional benefactor, i.e., his adoptive parents, since his natural parents remain responsible for him by law until the age of six. Furthermore, the natural parents continue to be liable for the basic needs of their child from the age of six to the extent that such needs are not or cannot be satisfied by the adopter: the continuation of this liability is based on the duty to give charity.

The right of inheritance is recognized according to *halakhah* as existing between a child and his natural parents only; for an adopted child the matter can be dealt with by means of testa- *Inheritance* mentary disposition, in which the adopter makes provision in his will for such portion of his estate to go to the child as the latter would have received by law, had the relationship been natural.

In accordance with the rule, "Scripture looks upon one who brings up an orphan as if he had begotten him", there is no halakhic objection to the adopter calling the adopted child his son and the latter calling the former his father. Hence, if these terms are used by either party in documents, where the adopter has no natural children and/or the child has no natural parents, they will be understood as referring to the adopter and the adopted, according to the general tenor of the document. *Naming the Child*

The act of adoption does not affect the laws of marriage and divorce. For example, although a brother and sister may not marry, two children adopted by one couple may marry each other, assuming no natural relationship exists between them. Similarly, a natural child may marry his or her adopted sister or brother. *Marriage and Divorce*

Problems of Adoption

Prospective parents were cautioned to establish the identity of their future child, for if the child were born of an incestuous relationship or of a married woman and a man other than her husband, he would be prohibited from later marrying any legitimate Jew.

No stigma of *mamzerut,* was, however, attached to non-Jewish children, even if they were born of an incestuous relationship. It was assumed, therefore, until recently, that a gentile child could be adopted, sometimes even in preference to Jewish children. *Gentile Child*

Adoption of a non-Jewish child often led to his conversion. Although conversion requires the consent of the individual, and a child does not have the legal capacity to consent, child conversion could be effected by an adult acting on behalf of the child because it is for the child's benefit. *Conversion*

80

Some Orthodox scholars oppose adoption of non-Jews because they no longer see conversion as a benefit. They explain that to be Jewish is beneficial only if the religious laws are kept *in toto;* to be a "sinning" Jew is not for the child's good; and today, when many adopting families do not observe the religious laws, the child will be brought up in this way. Therefore, because adoption may lead to conversion, and conversion cannot be effected properly, one should, according to this view, refrain from adopting non-Jews.

Procedure

Adopting procedures vary from place to place and country to country. Most places require consent of the natural parents and

A typical group of Jewish orphans found roaming about
Eastern Europe after World War I.

of the child, depending upon his age. A "Jewish adoption" is subject to the local adoption laws, and local agencies have been set up to aid prospective parents in adoptive procedures.

In the State of Israel, adoption severs all family ties between child and natural parent and creates new family ties between the child and his adoptive family as if the relationship were natural.

"Aurivius Family" by Jozef Israels.

Such adoption is granted only for persons under the age of eighteen, provided that the adopters are a minimum of eighteen years older than the prospective adoptee. The new relationship does not, however, change blood ties and the child will remain prohibited from marrying relatives of his natural parents while he will be permitted to marry adopted relatives.

The family unit of parents and adopted children need be no less cohesive than the natural family. The parents should provide their children with proper care, and the children should reciprocate with respect. Thus, although there is no formal obligation to do so, an adopted child should honor the parents that raised him by the recitation of *Kaddish* after their death, and perform in their lifetime all the necessary acts in connection with the command "Honor thy father and thy mother."

9. WOMEN

A woman of valor who can find?
For her price is far above rubies.
The heart of her husband doth safely trust in her . . .
She doeth him good and not evil
All the days of her life . . .
She riseth while it is yet night,
And giveth good to her household . . .
She considereth a field and buyeth it;
With the fruit of her hands she planteth a vineyard . . .
She stretcheth out her hand to the poor . . .
Strength and dignity are her clothing . . .
She openeth her mouth with wisdom . . .
And the law of lovingkindness is on her tongue . . .
Her children rise up and call her blessed;
Her husband also, and he praiseth her, saying:
'Many daughters have done valiantly, but thou excellest
*   them all'.*
Grace is deceitful, and beauty is vain;
But a woman that feareth the Lord, she will be praised.

Proverbs

This ideal as immortalized in Proverbs did not remain something of the past. Moritz Lazarus wrote in the 19th century, "In the days of horror of the later Roman Empire, throughout the time

83

of the migration of nations, it was not war alone that destroyed and annihilated all those peoples of which, despite their former world-dominating greatness, nothing remains but their name. It was rather the ensuing demoralization of home life. This is proved — it cannot be repeated too often — by the Jews; for they suffered more severely than any other nation; but, among them, the inmost living germ of morality — strict discipline and family devotion — was at all times preserved. This wonderful and mysterious preservation of the Jewish people is due to the Jewish woman. This is her glory, not alone in the history of her own people, but in the history of the world."

Obviously, in any discussion of the family, the position of the woman is of the utmost centrality. Jewish tradition sees the mother as the one who sets the tone of the home and who is the power behind her husband.

Both biblical and talmudic literature, however, depict varying attitudes toward women, not always as favorable as the above passage from the Book of Proverbs. References made to women's social, legal or religious status, written almost exclusively by men, reflect personal experiences, as well as recognition of the biological and functional differences between the sexes. Thus, "He who finds a woman finds good", but, "I find the woman more bitter than death". Whereas, it was generally agreed that a woman's testimony was not accepted in most cases, Rava (4th century Babylonian rabbi) not only accepted it in one case, but did so in the absence of the normal requirement of a second witness. In another case, Rava refuses to accept the testimony of Rav Papa, his colleague, on the grounds that supporting proof, i.e., a substantiating witness, was lacking. In modern rabbinic practice, women are generally accepted as witnesses. *Testimony*

A major difference between the role of the man and that of the woman in Jewish religious life concerns the performance of the commandments. The woman is commanded to observe all of the prohibitions, e.g., thou shalt not steal, just as is a man. She differs from the man, however, in that she is not required to perform those positive precepts which are to be performed at a specific time. For example, the commandment to honor one's father and mother is incumbent upon women because it applies at all times. However, since the recitation of some of the prayers is dependent on time, e.g., the morning prayers being said until one third of the day has passed, the woman is exempted from their performance. This does not mean that she is prohibited from observing such statutes, and in fact, some women do pray and there are even a few who put on *tefillin*, disregarding their exemption. *Religious Duties*

Commandments Based on Time

85

"The Blessing of the Candles" by Isidore Kaufman, Austria, 19th century. The blessing made at the inauguration of Sabbaths and festivals is a sanctification of the Jewish home (opposite).

Several explanations are given for this differentiation between men and women, none of which belittle the woman's position or give her inferior status. One eminent scholar wrote: "A careful examination of talmudic sources reveals that the Law's differentiation between men and woman was based on nature and natural function, and not on social or economic considerations. Now, nature has not endowed males with any 'built-in' apparatus for measuring time. In order that man learn

A ceramic wedding plate with the inscription "A woman of valor," Italy.

to sanctify time, the law ordains for him many commandments which are governed by a calendar and a clock. Women, on the other hand, by the very nature of their physical constitution and the requirements of the Law with regard to their menstrual periods, needed little more to make them aware of the sanctity of time." A simpler explanation for the woman's exemption is that she is normally very busy in the home, caring for her children, and is thus unable to be committed to any specific time.

86

Girls receiving instruction in the making of *ḥallah* for the Sabbath, 1970.

Moreover, the wording of the benediction recited each day in *Benediction* which a man praises God for not having made him a woman should not be overinterpreted since from the context it is clear that the thanks are for the greater opportunities a man has for carrying out the precepts. Notwithstanding, Claude Montefiore uses the benediction to state: "No amount of modern Jewish apologetic, endlessly poured forth, can alter the fact that the rabbinic attitude towards women was very different from our own. No amount of apologetics can get over the implication of the daily blessing, which Orthodox Judaism has still lacked the courage to remove from its official prayer book: 'Blessed art thou, O Lord our God, who hast not made me a woman.' At the same time it must be readily admitted that the rabbis seemed to have loved their wives, that they all, apparently, had only one wife each, and that the position of the wife was one of much influence and importance."

According to talmudic law a woman can be called up to the *Reading of the* reading of the Torah Scroll in the synagogue; however, because *Law* of the "honor of the congregation," they were not. One possible explanation of the term "honor of the congregation" is the fact that in talmudic times and before, each individual who was called to the reading, himself read the portion to which he was called. Thus, in order not to embarrass the men who could not do so — the reading requiring a special skill — women were not called. The Reconstructionist and Reform movements have reinstituted the practice of calling women to the Torah, and Hebrew Union College has ordained the first woman rabbi, who is now serving in a synagogue pulpit.

Another difference between the sexes exists in the life cycle ceremonies. Almost all of the post-natal ceremonies pertain only to a male child. Indeed, the Falashas of Ethiopia who are considered by some to be of Jewish descent, practice female circumcision, but this is not ordained in the Bible or later codes, and is not practiced by any other Jewish sect or movement. Except for one minority opinion, which requires a female firstborn to fast on the day preceding Passover as part of the general fast of firstborns, there is no special status attached to the birth of a girl.

Glückel of Hameln, married at 14 and mother of 12 children, she advised her husband on all financial matters and very successfully ran his business affairs after his death. She wrote her memoirs which are an important source for Central European Jewish history.

"Judith and Holofernes" by Andrea Mantagna, Padua, 1495. The Book of Judith, an apocryphal work, tells how the beautiful Judith saved her town and its Jews. She beguiled and later beheaded the commander of the besieging army.

The significance of a female birth, according to one interpretation of a talmudic aphorism, was that it was a positive sign that the next child might well be a boy.

However, although a girl's birth is not surrounded by a *The Homem* ceremony, her future is nonetheless important. She would someday be the bearer of children, and she would be the homemaker. This latter responsibility was a most difficult and delicate one. It included providing an atmosphere in which the children could understand and live a Jewish life, clothing the family, supervising the kitchen, i.e., knowledge of the dietary laws, as well as knowledge of the home rituals. It was her responsibility to bring up the younger children and see to their education (see page 20, 96, 100) together with her husband.

Women, by talmudic legislation, were exempt from the *Study* precept of studying Torah, and as a result few women were learned. The saying that women acquire merit by sending their sons to study and encouraging their husbands to study is very revealing in this connection. However, a dramatic change has occurred and today even the daughters of the ultra-Orthodox receive an education including among other subjects the study of Torah.

Legally the woman's status was not much better than her being "owned" by her husband and by biblical law, a man can divorce his wife with or without her consent. Rabbenu Gershom (10th/11th century), however, enacted an ordinance, now accepted throughout almost all of the Jewish world, whereby a woman had to consent to a divorce. The same ordinance prohibited polygamy which is permitted according to biblical and talmudic law.

The comparisons of the love of God for Israel to the love of *Divorce* husband for wife, spoken by the prophets, can only have been made to a society in which women were respected. Similarly, many talmudic passages relate the high regard for women. Rabbi Joseph hearing his mother's footsteps in the early morning hours, said: "Let me arise before the approach of the *Shekhinah* (Divine Presence)." The redemption of Israel from Egypt was said to have been by virtue of the righteous women of the time. Women were pictured as having greater faith than men and greater powers of discernment, and they are especially tenderhearted. The Torah, the greatest joy of the rabbis, is frequently hypostatized as a woman and is represented as God's daughter and Israel's bride.

The Midrash depicts the woman as follows: "God said: 'I will not create her from the head (of Adam) lest she hold up her head too proudly; nor from the eye lest she be a coquette; nor from the ear lest she be an eavesdropper; nor from the mouth lest she be too talkative; nor from the heart lest she be too jealous; nor from the hand lest she be too acquisitive; nor from the foot lest she be a gadabout; but from a part of the body which is hidden (from the rib) in order that she should be modest.' " Apparently it didn't work, and in another midrashic passage, several negative qualities are ascribed to women. They are: greedy, eavesdroppers, lazy, and jealous; they are also querrulous, and garrulous. A talmudic passage reads, that of "ten measures of speech which descended to the world, women took nine." *A Midrashic Interpretation*

Whatever the attitude, women have played important roles, not only in the shaping of the home and thereby history, but in determining the destiny of the Jewish people. The Matriarch, Sarah, told Abraham to send his son, Ishmael, away, whereby Isaac became the sole heir. The reluctant Abraham was told by God to obey Sarah's wish. Rebekah was instrumental in obtaining Isaac's partriarchal blessing for her son, Jacob, instead of Esau. Miriam the sister of Moses was a prophetess in her own right and was consulted on important matters. Deborah the Judge stands out for her leadership in a confrontation with the Canaanite enemies and in the reign of Josiah (640–609 b.c.e.), Huldah the prophetess was consulted on matters of state. A later example in the field of economics, Gracia Nasi, (c. 1510–1569) a *Famous Women*

Marrano and one of the richest people of her day, must be mentioned. She returned to Judaism and used her wealth and influence to assist the survival of the Jews in one of the most turbulent periods of their history. In religion as well women held positions of esteem; some were even ḥasidic rabbis, e.g., Perele, daughter of Israel of Kozienice; Sarah, daughter of Joshua Heschel Teomim—Fraenkel; "Malkele the Triskerin"; and Hannah Rachel, the "Maid of Ludomir." This is but a short list. Women's influence is not limited to any one age or period, but extends as far back as the beginnings of the people and stretches up to the present. It is interesting that a child is considered Jewish irrespective of father's religion; it is the Jewish mother who makes the child Jewish.

Sepia drawing by Rembrandt of Jael slaying the Canaanite General Sisera (Judges 4-5; opposite). Woman on guard against Arab attack at one of the "Stockade and Watchtower" settlements built overnight, Palestine,1936 (right). Israel Defense Forces Sergeant teaching Hebrew to new immigrants from Kurdistan (below).

Mrs. Golda Meir, Prime Minister of the State of Israel, receiving the key to New York City from Mayor John V. Lindsay during her visit there in 1969.

In the State of Israel, women have been given equal status with men in many respects. The Declaration of Independence ensures complete equality of social and political rights to all inhabitants, irrespective of sex. The Womens Equal Rights Law of 1951 guarantees women equal legal status in all matters other than personal status, i.e., marriage and divorce, which is governed by religious law. The Equal Rights Law is an obvious outcome of the status women enjoyed prior to statehood when they were an integral part of the defense of the country. To measure the effectiveness of the Law, one need only observe that, after only twenty years of statehood, the government selected as its head a woman, Prime Minister Golda Meir.

Henrietta Szold wrote: "Jewish custom bids the Jewish mother, after her preparations for the Sabbath have been completed on Friday evening, kindle the Sabbath Lamp. That is symbolic of the Jewish woman's influence on her own home, and through it upon larger circles. She is the inspirer of a pure, chaste family life whose hallowing influences are incalculable; she is the center of all spiritual endeavors, the confidante and fosterer of every undertaking. To her the talmudic sentence applies: 'It is women alone through whom God's blessings are vouchsafed to a house'."

10. THE INTERMEDIATE YEARS

When Israel stood before Mount Sinai to receive the Torah, the Holy One, blessed be He, said to them: 'Shall I give you the Torah? Bring me good sureties that you will keep it, and then I will give it to you.' They replied: 'Sovereign of the Universe, our ancestors will be our guarantors.' . . . Said God to them: 'I have faults to find in your ancestors . . . Bring me therefore good sureties and I will give it to you.' They then said: 'Sovereign of the Universe, our prophets will be our sureties.' He replied: 'I have faults to find with them,' . . . They said to Him: 'Our children shall be our sureties.' To which God replied: 'In truth, these are good sureties; for their sake I will give it to you.'

Midrash to Song of Songs

From infancy to adulthood the child's life is marked by rapid changes. Besides his physical growth, he learns to adapt himself to society, his general knowledge increases, and he begins to formulate his own ideas. Jewish scholars have placed great emphasis on the importance of study and mental growth in the intermediate years, from the cradle to majority.

Family Education

Whereas the Bible does not command the organization of educational institutions on a group, tribal, or national level, it does speak of the family educational unit. Every Jewish parent is instructed, "And you shall teach them (the words of God) to your children . . . in order that you lengthen your days and your children's days upon the earth . . . " The children, too, are instructed, "Remember the days of old, consider the years of

In the Bible

95

ages past, ask your father, he will inform you, your elders, they will tell you." Of interest is the almost identical repetition of biblical passages, "and you shall tell your son " and, "and if your son should ask, then tell him", which prompted commentators to point out that the parental obligation of educating the young does not apply only when the child shows an interest or when he is intelligent enough to ask, but rather a parent must, in all instances, inculcate the young with a sense of history and involvement with his people.

In order to organize the Jewish home as an educational insti- *Family* tution, the interrelationships of the members of the family were *Interrelation* clearly defined, thus ensuring the proper atmosphere for love and respect, important ingredients in the process of transmission.

The rituals in the Bible, performed by the parents are a *Ritual* method of instruction for the children and supplement the child's oral and book learning. The celebration of holidays, commemorating Jewish religious and historical events, becomes a primary means of conveying cultural values from one generation to another and the performance of the daily commandments, both biblical and rabbinic, such as prayer, phylacteries, blessings over food, *kashrut* and ritual cleanliness, in addition to their intrinsic value, are intended to instill the child with a reverence for God, the ultimate purpose of education.

Method of Instruction
However much emphasis the Bible placed on education, the *In the Bible* masses were most probably virtually ignorant of all but the practical application of the law. The theory, system and development of the law as it should be applied to new problems and needs was only known to the leaders, such as Moses, Joshua and their counterparts in the Monarchy as well as to a handful of "elders". According to the Talmud, a system of mass education did exist in the time of Moses, but it is doubtful whether more than a very basic outline of the law and its practice was taught to

96

"The Examination" by Moritz Oppenheim. A common scene in the traditional Jewish home, the grandfather (or father) reviews what the child has learned while the mother looks on admiringly (opposite).

the people as a whole. Moses was taught the law by God, after which he instructed Aaron, his brother and High Priest. When Aaron understood the law, he would sit to Moses' left, whereupon Aaron's sons entered the tent to receive instruction from Moses. Moses' explanation to them having been completed, and their having assumed the proper positions to the sides of Moses and Aaron, the elders were instructed and following them the masses. It is questionable, however, whether this method was often used. On one biblical verse concerning Moses' obligation to transmit his knowledge of the Sabbath laws to the people, he is told "and you shall speak to the people," on which the Mekhilta comments that whereas in most instances Moses could choose to

delegate the responsibility of teaching to others, in the case of the Sabbath laws he was required to present the material himself.

Although there were public gatherings at which the law was expounded — Ezra's convocations and the yearly *Hakhel* ceremony at which the king read passages of the Bible are examples — it was, to a large extent, the family that transmitted the heritage. With time, because of the growing complexities of life and the expanded boundaries of religious study, education passed from the family to the school and trained personnel. Joshua ben Gamla, a first century High Priest, is credited with having devised a system of education and ensured the continuation of Torah study: "Truly, the name of that man (Joshua) is blessed . . . since but for him the Torah would have been forgotten in Israel." He evolved a system whereby "teachers of young children be appointed in each district and each town" whereas previously they were to be found only in Jerusalem. In addition he laid down sound pedagogical principles to be used in Torah instruction.

However, there can be no doubt that the family performance of rituals remained the most effective educational experience. The lighting of the Hanukkah lamp, although incumbent on the head of the household alone, was not uncommonly performed by parent and child alike. At an early age the child accompanied his father to the synagogue for prayer; the *Kiddush* ritual over a cup of wine, inaugurating the Sabbath or festivals was practiced by children as well as the father. A daughter, together with her mother, would pronounce the blessing over the Sabbath lights and assist with the preparation of foods, learning the laws of *kashrut* as well as the Jewish cuisine. The Sabbath, on which no work was permitted, gave the entire family an opportunity to enjoy each other's company, and especially today, in a highly mechanized world, reconfirms family togetherness. The Sabbath is often spent in study, with father questioning the child on the week's work at school or with a discussion on the portion of the

Bible read in the synagogue that morning. The annual highlight of the family's educational experience is Passover at which time elaborate preparation for, and participation in the *seder* service, prompted interest even in the youngest of children. All the rituals were important components of Judaism, but their importance was magnified in each instance when children were present and could be instructed in their performance.

A lesson on family education can be learned from the passage of the Bible: "If a man have a stubborn and rebellious son, that will not hearken to the voice of his father and the voice of his mother and though they chasten him, will not hearken unto them, then shall his father and his mother lay hold of him and bring him out unto the elders of his city . . . They shall say unto the elders of his city, 'This our son is stubborn and rebellious, he doth not hearken to our voice, he is a glutton and a drunkard.' And all the men of his city shall stone him with stones that he die; so shalt thou put away the evil from the midst of thee; and all Israel shall hear, and fear." *Rebellious Son*

Interpreting every word of the biblical text restrictively, the talmudic jurists reduced the practicability of this law to nil and indeed the sages stated that "there never has been and never will be a case of the rebellious son." For example, the term "son" implies that if the child is a man, i.e., his pubic hair has grown, he does not fit the category. The term also excludes a daughter though daughters are no less apt to be rebellious. The son must also be thirteen years of age or else he cannot bear criminal responsibility. He may, therefore, only be indicted during a maximum period of six months, or according to some, three months. Furthermore, as father and mother have to be "defied", to "take hold of him," to "say" to the elders, and to show them "this" is our son, neither of them may be deaf, dumb, blind, lame, or crippled, or else the law does not apply. It becomes clear from the interpretation of the phrase "he doth not hearken to our voice," that the passage was intended not for practical applica- *Parental Harmony* tion, but for educational and deterrent purposes only. The sages explain: the phrase not having ended with the plural 'voices' implies that both father's and mother's "voice" must be of the same pitch and tonal quality. This means that when a father's instructions to the child differ from those of the mother, i.e., their 'voices' are different, any fault in the son's actions is to be attributed to them and the son cannot be held responsible for his misdeeds. It is only when in harmony, father and mother together lead and instruct the child that they can then be released from their responsibility.

The biblical text then is a warning to parents, as one seventeenth century sage writes: "In our times, we pay no attention to gluttonous and defiant sons, and everybody covers up the sins of his children; even where they might be liable to flogging or to

capital punishment under the law; they are not even reprimanded. Many such children are leading purposeless lives and learn nothing — and we know that Jerusalem was destroyed because children loafed around and did not study." Through rebuke, reproof, and proper influence the intention of the Bible could be fulfilled, i.e., not to bring a defiant son to justice, but ensure that there would be no need for such drastic measures.

In this exercise in interpretation the rabbinic sages were stressing what has become accepted, in modern times, as a sound principle of education. The spirit and atmosphere of the home are the main factors in ensuring the growth of well-adjusted children, and the rebellious son is in fact the product of a broken or disturbed home. The amazingly low incidence of juvenile delinquency in Jewish communities — at least until the modern age of complete emancipation — is surely an indication of the value of Jewish traditional home life. In the ideal Jewish home there is a sense of security created by the fact that each member knows his role, the child is aware of what is expected of him, and knows that he can rely on his parents and siblings for any support he may need.

By its very nature, the traditional Jewish way of life ensures *Family Solidarity* that parents spent time with their children. Sabbaths and holidays are something to look forward to with eager expectation; they in fact become family experiences with each member contributing his part. The common interest of all the members of the family in maintaining and developing a special way of life adds an element of idealism to what is otherwise humdrum existence. Example on the part of the parents is also of immense importance. When the wider family group lives together or in close proximity the child has the opportunity of seeing how his father and mother honor their own parents — this is often denied in the complexities of urban life today. All in all, the advances of modern technology seem to have had a destructive effect on the cohesiveness of the family unit: the benefits of modern mobility

101

"Hasidim in the Beth Midrash" by Isidore Kaufman. The children are seen praying with their fathers (opposite).

and the availability of cheap sources of entertainment have robbed the family of its position of centrality in the life of the individual.

A familiar biblical admonition to observe the precepts is followed by the promise: "in order that your days and the days of your sons be prolonged upon the land . . . " For a family that overcomes the challenges and strains of twentieth-century life, and succeeds in cultivating the relationships hallowed by Jewish

"The Rabbi's Blessing" by Moritz Oppenheim. The father looks on as his child is blessed by the rabbi (left). Drawing by Jacob Epstein of Eastern European immigrants in New York City (right).

traditional practice, the above-quoted biblical promise need not be merely a reward for having taught one's sons. It is, rather, the logical consequence of sound education.

11. BAR MITZVAH AND BAT MITZVAH

O My God, and God of My Fathers,
On this solemn and sacred day, which marketh my passage from boyhood to manhood, I humbly venture to raise my eyes unto Thee, and to declare with sincerity and truth that henceforth I will observe all Thy commandments, and undertake to bear the responsibility of all mine actions towards Thee. In my earliest infancy I was brought within Thy sacred covenant with Israel, and today I again enter as an active responsible member the pale of Thine elect congregation, in the midst of which I will never cease to glorify Thy holy name in the face of all nations.

Benjamin Artom

Preparation
Religious education, both in family and institutional form should begin at an early age. "From when must a father begin to teach his son? From the time the boy begins to talk, the father begins teaching him by saying: 'Moses commanded us the Law, an inheritance of the Congregation of Jacob' followed by the first verse of the Shema ('Hear O Israel, The Lord is Our God, the Lord is One'), after which he continues to teach him little by little until the boy reaches the age of six or seven at which time he is taken to a 'teacher for the young'." It is written in the law codes, "Immediately after the child's third birthday, he is taught the letters of the Torah (i.e., the Hebrew alphabet) in order that

103

he should acquaint himself with reading the Torah." So important is instruction of the young that one may not interrupt the study "even in order to build the Temple (in Jerusalem)."

Study is not limited to the young: "Every Jew is commanded to study Torah, whether poor or rich, whether physically fit or handicapped, whether young or old." There is, however, a difference between the young and the old. The young, i.e., children before puberty, are not themselves commanded to study; it is the father's obligation to see that they are given a proper education. After puberty, however, the child is responsible to provide his own education; a boy becomes an adult at *bar mitzvah* and a girl at *bat mitzvah*.

Study

Change of Status
Whereas puberty does not necessarily occur at exactly the same time in everyone, Jewish law has fixed the age of thirteen years and one day for a boy, and twelve years and one day for a girl as the beginning of adulthood. Therefore, a child legally enters the stage of puberty and becomes *bar* or *bat mitzvah* at that time, whether or not there is evidence of physical maturity. At this age young people were thought to be able to control their desires, a manifestation of adulthood. Furthermore, until puberty the child's actions reflect what he has been taught and what he has seen without interjecting his own interpretation. From puberty, the actions of the child begin to reflect his own understanding; he questions the right and wrong that until now he had accepted as truth simply because his parents had told him so. The Midrash records that changes in biblical figures occured at puberty. Abraham is said to have rejected his father's idolatry at this age, and at thirteen Jacob and his twin brother Esau went their separate ways — Jacob to study Torah and Esau to worship idols. One talmudic commentator however, sought no justification or explanation for choosing the age of thirteen, claiming that it was set by "Moses at Sinai."

Puberty

A *Bar Mitzvah* in the ancient synagogue at Masada (top). Leaders of the Bukharan community in Jerusalem, 1928. The two boys are dressed in traditional *Bar Mitzvah* cloaks (center). Israel Defense Minister Moshe Dayan speaking at *Bar Mitzvah* celebration of boys whose fathers were killed in the Six-Day War. The celebration was held at Kefar Ḥabad, 1970 (below).

The Bar Mitzvah Ceremony

Although Judaism usually celebrates important events in the life cycle, *bar mitzvah* was not always accompanied by a ceremony. The first mention of a ceremony is in the fifteenth century. A special celebration for a girl, the *bat mitzvah,* is not mentioned before the nineteenth century.

The *bar mitzvah* ceremony in its basic form consists of calling up the boy to the public reading of the Torah on the first occasion that it is read following his thirteenth birthday according to the Jewish calendar. This is the first public demonstration of the boy's new role as a full member of the community. The boy's father is also called to the reading of the Law, after which he recites the benediction: "Blessed is He Who has now freed me from the responsibility of this one." Among the Jews of Eastern Europe the boy was usually called up to the Torah on the Monday or Thursday following his birthday. In Western Europe the occasion took on a more ceremonial importance, and it was customary for the boy to be honored on the Sabbath, when he himself would read the final portion of the Law and the portion from the prophets *(Haftarah).* According to an old Ashkenazi custom in Lithuania and Erez Israel, the boy recited the last portion of the Law on the Sabbath preceding his birthday and would then receive an ordinary honor on the Sabbath following his birthday. In the seventeenth and eighteenth centuries the custom was recorded at Worms, Germany, that those boys who were able and had pleasing voices conducted parts or all of the service. In some communities it was, and still is, customary for a young man, after much preparation, to read the whole Torah portion of that Sabbath. Among the Jews of Morocco a special *piyyut* (hymn) was recited when a *bar mitzvah* was called up to the Torah, and, in most places, a special invocation is made at the end of the reading for the boy and his family.

On a Sabbath when a *bar mitzvah* is celebrated, the morning service assumes a more festive atmosphere. Members of the boy's family are also called up to the reading of the Torah, and a special sermon is frequently delivered by the rabbi, stressing the responsibilities that are attached to the boy's new status. In many modern synagogues, the rabbi concludes his sermon by invoking the priestly blessing or other blessing, and the boy is given a gift from the congregation. After the service, a festive *kiddush* (meal or refreshments, including wine) is often held, with a banquet on the same or following day. Some authorities ruled that parents must arrange a banquet when their son becomes *bar mitzvah* just as they must on the day of his wedding.

It was customary for the boy to deliver a talmudic discourse at the banquet. The discourse, known to Sephardim as the *"tefillin derashah"*, frequently served as an occasion for the boy to thank his parents for their love and care, and the guests for their participation in his celebration. The custom is still observed today, with sons of traditional families giving a talmudic discourse, and others a more general talk. In Conservative, Reform, and some Orthodox synagogues, the boy recites a prayer before the Ark of the Law in place of the discourse. *Discourse*

The major ritual innovation obligatory on a boy of thirteen is that henceforth he is required to put on *tefillin* for the morning prayers. He is usually coached in the forms of the rite some time prior to his birthday. In many places, the boy begins wearing the *tefillin* one month before his birthday. The Ḥabad school of Ḥasidism teaches that boys begin two months in advance, one month without reciting the benediction and the second month with the blessing. Other Ḥasidim, as well as Sephardim, however, insist that *tefillin* should not be worn before the actual date of majority. *Tefillin*

The Bat Mitzvah Ceremony
The ceremony for a girl, *bat mitzvah,* was officially introduced in France and Italy and widely adopted in other countries. Forms

of the ceremony differ widely, ranging from having the girl recite the portion from the prophets and conduct specific prayers in the synagogue, to confining the entire celebration to the home or school. In many Israeli Orthodox synagogues the *bat mitzvah* is celebrated by calling the girl's father and brothers to the Torah; a special sermon is preached, and the girl is presented with a gift. In many congregations a collective ceremony is held when girls have reached the proper age. In recent times, the *bat mitzvah* has often been celebrated not as a religious ceremony but as a birthday celebration and family occasion.

Most congregational Hebrew schools have special classes for the preparation of boys and girls for *bar* and *bat mitzvah*. In some congregations, the boy is not allowed to celebrate his *bar mitzvah* until he passes an examination in Hebrew on the fundamentals of the Jewish religion.

Confirmation

In Reform congregations the confirmation ceremony occupies an important place. This was originally introduced, in the nineteenth century German Reform as a substitute for *bar mitzvah*. The ceremony was held at a later age, sixteen or seventeen, on the grounds that before that age the child cannot adequately understand the implications of the rituals. In modern times, especially in the United States, confirmation has been adopted by Reform and Conservative congregations as a ceremony additional to *bar mitzvah,* although still a number of years later. The main intention of the confirmation ceremony is to prolong the period of a child's Jewish education, and it is usually celebrated with a "class" of young people being confirmed at the same time. The ceremony is usually held on or about the festival of Shavuot, the festival commemorating the receiving of the Law (coinciding with the end of the school year). The confirmands recite various sections from Scriptures and publicly declare their devotion to Judaism. The boys and girls frequently receive a special certificate, testifying to their acceptance into the Jewish community.

Legal Status

Whether or not a ceremony takes place at its proper time, the child's legal position changes. For example, heretofore he received the merit of the father or could suffer for his parent's sins; his vows were meaningless and he had no legal capacity. After *bar* or *bat mitzvah* all rights, privileges, and obligations of an adult devolve upon him. His business transactions are valid, he can act as an agent in all matters, he can become a member of a court and a boy can be counted as part of a *minyan* (the quorum of ten men necessary for communal prayer). Yet there are notable exceptions, e.g., the testimony of a thirteen year old is not accepted concerning matters of real estate because he is not yet "knowledgeable about buying and selling."

The Future

After *bar mitzvah,* except for marriage, the Jew is not the subject of any other personal ceremony. However, his life as a Jew is characterized by several stages, just as his life has been a series of developments till that time. Birth, circumcision, and *pidyon ha-ben* (redemption of the firstborn) have been followed by study and *bar mitzvah.* The next years are marked by continued study, marriage, and the pursuit of wisdom. As the Mishnah has it: "At five years the age is reached for the study of Scripture, at ten for the study of the Mishnah, at thirteen for the fulfillment of the commandments, at fifteen for the study of the Talmud, at eighteen for marriage, at twenty for seeking a livelihood, at thirty for entering one's full strength, at forty for understanding, at fifty for counsel, at sixty a man attains old age, at seventy the hoary head, at eighty the gift of special strength, at ninety he bends beneath the weight of years, at a hundred he is as if he were already dead and had passed away from the world."

"Conclusion of the Sabbath" by Moritz Oppenheim, Germany, 1866. The entire family is gathered around as the father pours the wine and the youngest child holds the *Havdalah* candle.

GLOSSARY

Ger, originally used for strangers living among the tribes of Israel, it is presently used for all proselytes to Judaism.

Halakhah, Jewish law.

Hanukkah, eight-day celebration starting the twenty-fifth day of the month Kislev (December) commemorating the victory of Judah Maccabee over the Syrian king Antiochus Epiphanes and the subsequent rededication of the Temple.

Ḥasid (pl. Ḥasidîm), adherents of religious movement (Ḥasidism) founded in first half of the 18th century.

Kaddish, liturgical poem. One of the forms is recited by mourners in memory of the dead.

Kashrut, Jewish dietary laws.

Kohen (pl. *Kohanim*), priest, descendant of Aaron, Moses' brother.

Mamzer, illegitimate child born of an adulterous or incestuous relationship.

Mekhilta, halakhic Midrash.

Mezuzot, parchment scroll with selected Torah verses placed in container and affixed to doorposts of rooms occupied by Jews.

Midrash, collection of rabbinic interpretations of, and homilies on, the Bible.

Mishnah, earliest codification of Jewish oral law; completed in 3rd century c.e.

Mitzvah, biblical or rabbinic injunction; applied also to good or charitable deeds.

Mohel (pl. *mohalim*), official performing circumcisions.

Passover, a spring festival, beginning on the 15th of the month of Nisan, lasting seven days in Israel and eight days in the Diaspora, commemorating the Exodus from Egypt.

Seder, the ceremony on the first night (in the Diaspora first two nights) of Passover.

Sephardi (pl. Sephardim), Jew(s) of Spain and Portugal and their descendants, wherever resident.

She-heḥeyanu, benediction of thanksgiving.

Talmud, compendium of discussion on the Mishnah by generations of scholars and jurists in many academies over a period of centuries.

Tefillin, phylacteries, worn by male Jews during weekday morning service.

Ẓaddik, person outstanding for his faith and piety.

ABBREVIATION OF SOURCES

BIBLE[1]

Gen.	– Genesis	Josh.	– Joshua	Mic.	– Micah
Ex.	– Exodus	Jud.	– Judges	Ps.	– Psalms
Lev.	– Leviticus	Sam.	– Samuel	Prov.	– Proverbs
Num.	– Numbers	Is.	– Isaiah	Ecc.	– Ecclesiastes
Deut.	– Deuteronomy	Jer.	– Jeremiah	Esth.	– Esther
		Ezek.	– Ezekiel	Macc.	– Maccabees

TALMUD[2]

TJ	– Jerusalem Talmud[3]				
BB	– *Bava Batra*	Hul.	– *Hullin*	San.	– *Sanhedrin*
Bek.	– *Bekhorot*	Ket.	– *Ketubbot*	Shab.	– *Shabbat*
Ber.	– *Berakhot*	Kid.	– *Kiddushin*	Shev.	– *Shevuot*
BK.	– *Bava Kama*	Meg.	– *Megillah*	Sot.	– *Sotah*
Eruv.	– *Eruvin*	Ned.	– *Nedarim*	Suk.	– *Sukkah*
Git.	– *Gittin*	Nid.	– *Niddah*	Ta'an.	– *Ta'anit*
Hor.	– *Horiot*	Oho.	– *Oholot*	Yev.	– *Yevamot*

LATER AUTHORITIES

Yad	– Maimonides, *Yad Ḥazakah*
Sh.Ar.	– *Shulḥan Arukh*
EH	– *Even ha-Ezer*
HM	– *Ḥoshen Mishpat*
OH	– *Orah Ḥayyim*
YD	– *Yoreh De'ah*

---

[1] All biblical abbreviations followed by R. (e.g., Gen. R.) will refer to the Midrash –
e.g., Genesis Rabbah, Ruth Rabba

[2] References to the Mishnah are in the form Nid. 4:1 (i.e., *Tractate Niddah*, chapter 4,
Mishnah 1); references to the Gemara are in the form Nid. 12b (i.e., *Tractate
Niddah*, page 12, side b). Thus a reference Nid. 4:1, 12b will first refer to the
Mishnah and then to the Gemara.

[3] Otherwise Talmud references are to the Babylonian Talmud.

page

1   *All Israelites . . .* – Lev. R. 4:6

1   "My ancestor is greater . . . " – San. 4:5

4   "a learned bastard . . . " – Hor. 3:8

4   ten social groups – Kid. 4:1

6   "anyone with a . . . stigma . . . " – Kid. 70b

6   "When two people . . . " – Kid. 71b

6   "When the Holy One . . . " – Kid. 70b

6   "The Holy One is reluctant . . . " – Gen. R. 82:11; cf. TJ Suk. 5:8

7   "anyone taking a wife . . . " – Kid. 70a

7   "Judaism insists that man . . . " – see Hertz, J.H., *A Book of Jewish Thoughts,* p. 198

8   "The old Jewish doctrine . . . " – see Hertz, J.H., *A Book of Jewish Thoughts,* p. 198

8   "All Israelites . . . " – San. 27b; Shev. 39a

10   *Now the Lord said . . .* – Gen. 12:1–3

10   "The Jew's home . . . " – Hertz, J.H., *A Book of Jewish Thought,* p. 11

10   Elkanah – I Sam. 1

10   Michal – I Sam. 19

11   Sons of Jacob – Gen. 44:18–45:3

12   Rashi – Rashi to Gen. 22:6–8

13   King Solomon – I Kings 3:22–27

14   Jacob and Esau – Gen. 32

14   Joseph . . . Reuben – Gen. 37:18–22

14   Miriam . . . Moses – Ex. 2:43

14   Dinah . . . Shechem – Gen. 34

15   Rachel . . . Akiva – Ket. 62b; Ned. 50a

15   "Who is wealthy? . . . " – Shab. 25b

15   Beruryah – Midrash to Prov. 31:1

16   blood relatives – Lev. 18 and 20

17   ritual . . . testing – Num. 5

17   inheritance . . . daughters – Num. 26:28–34, 27:1–11, 36:10–12; Josh. 17:1–6

17   divorce . . . die childless – Deut. 24 and 25

17   Decalogue – Ex. 20

17   Dama – Kid. 31a

page

19   father . . . head − Num. 8:54; Gen. 24:38, 46:31

19   "master" − Gen. 20:2; Ex. 21:3; Lev. 21:4; Deut. 24:4

19   He "took" her . . . − Gen. 29, 34:16; Ex. 22:16; Deut. 22:29; Ruth 4:10

19   determine . . . spouse − Josh. 15:16; I Sam. 18:17, 19, 21, 27, 25:44

19   show . . . love . . . pity − Gen. 25:28, 37:4; Ps. 103:13

19   concubine − Gen. 16:1−2, 29:15−30

19   two wives of equal − Gen. 26:34, 28:9; I Sam 1:2

20   woman . . . head . . . household − II Kings 8:1−6

20   Sarah − Gen. 21:12

20   Manoah − Jud. 13:23

20   Rebekah . . . Leah . . . Rachel − Gen. 27:5, 30:16, 31:34

20   care and love − Gen. 25:28; Is. 49:15, 66:13; Prov. 4:3

20   father . . . teach − Kid. 40a

20   favoritism − Shab. 10b

20   "A man . . . spend . . . " − Hul. 84b

20   childlessness − Gen. 30:23; I Sam. 1

20   children . . . family name − Ps. 127:3−5; Num. 27:4, 8

20   mother . . . father . . . instructing − Prov. 1−8; Gen. 18:19; Ex. 12:26−27

21   mother . . . until marriage − Mic. 7:6

21   "Honor thy father . . . " − Ex. 20:15; Lev. 20:9; Deut. 27:16

21   "In thee . . . made light . . . " − Ezek. 22:7; see also Mic. 7:6; Prov. 20:20

22   sell . . . slavery . . . prostitution − Ex. 21:7−11; Lev. 19:29

22   vows . . . damages − Num. 30:40; Ex. 22:15−16

22   return . . . father's − Gen. 38:11; Lev. 22:13; Ruth 1:15

22   "brother" . . . "sister" − Gen. 4:2, 20:12, 43:7; Lev. 18:9, 20:17

22   Laban − Gen. 24

23   Brotherly solidarity − Prov. 17:17

23   "Behold how good . . . " − Ps. 133:1

23   obligated to avenge − Num. 35:19−28; Deut. 19:6; II Sam. 3:27

23   ransom − Lev. 25:48; Ps. 49:8

23   nephews, fellow tribesmen . . . − Gen. 13:8; Lev. 21:10; Deut. 2:4, 8, 23:8

24   "In the narrow . . . " − see Hertz, J.H., *A Book of Jewish Thoughts,* p. 10

24   *Your question . . .* − see Hertz, J.H., *A Book of Jewish Thoughts,* p. 26

26   Egyptians . . . Ammonites − Deut. 23:4, 9

26   "Entreat me not . . . " − Ruth 1:16

26   Midrash . . . Naomi . . . − Ruth R. 2:22, 23

27   "Is this all the love . . . " − Gen. R. 70:5

114

page

27   "He loveth the stranger . . . " — Deut. 10:18

28   Rabbi Simeon — Mekhilta, *Nezikim (Mishpatim)* 18

28   'and those that are beloved . . . ' — Jud. 5:31

28   "Whoever befriends . . . " — Gen. R. 84:4

28   "Proselytes who converted . . . " — Yev. 24b

29   "Do not have any faith . . . " — Midrash Ruth Zuta 1:2

29   Golden Calf — Ex. R. 42:6

29   Maimonides — Responsa Rambam (ed., Friedman), no. 42 and no. 369

31   Moses Feinstein — Iggerot Moshe, YD, no. 160

32   "so that they should not say . . . " — Yev. 22a; Yad, *Issurei Bi'ah* 14:12

32   male . . . female proselyte — Kid. 73a, 78a; Yev. 60b

33   *I will continue* . . . — see Hertz, J.H., *A Book of Jewish Thoughts,* p. 4

33   Pregnancy . . . — Nid. 30b–31b

38   "If a woman . . . " — Lev. 12:2

42   Astrology — Shab. 156a as translated by Soncino, *The Babylonian Talmud, Seder Mo'ed,* vol. 1, p. 799

43   sexual relations . . . — Lev. 12:1–8; Sh. Ar., YD 194

46   *To everything* . . . — Ecc. 3:1–4

46   pains and perils — Gen. 3:16

46   prophets — Jer. 6:24, 22:23, 49:24, 50:43; Mic. 4:9–10

46   Rachel . . Eli . . Michal — Gen. 35:18; I Sam 4:20; San. 21a

46   Mishnah . . . death — Shab. 2:6

46   "And if men . . ." — Ex. 21:22–23

48   "He that smiteth . . ." — Ex. 21:12; BK 42a

48   abortion . . . not punishable — Mekhilta, *Mishpatim* 4; see San. 84b and Nid. 44b

48   one day old — Nid. 5:3

48   gentile — San. 57b

48   abortion . . . prohibited — Tosafot to San. 59a; Hul. 33a; Yev. 62b; Nid. 13a, 31a

48   Josephus — Josephus, *Apion* 2:202

48   "if a woman . . . labor . . . " — Oho. 7:6

48   'it may be killed . . . " She (the mother) . . . " — San. 72b

49   "such (difficulty . . ." — Yad, *Roze'aḥ* 1:9

49   "one does not know . . . " — TJ San. 8:9

49   "for even if . . ." — Meiri to San. 72b

49   "because . . . pursuing . . . " — Yad, *Roze'aḥ* 1:9

page

49   mother's illness — *Paḥad Yiẓḥak, s.v. Nefalim*

49   illness not been caused — Responsa Maharit, no. 99

49   Jacob Emden — *She'elot* Yaveẓ 1:43

49   Benzion Uziel — *Mishpetei Uziel*, 2, no. 47

49   Ephraim Oshey — *Mi-Ma'amakim*, no. 20

50   Later responsum — *Leḥem ha-Panim*, last *Kunteres*, no. 19

51   emotional or mental — Unterman in No'am, 6(1963), 1–11; Zwieg in No'am, 7(1964), 36–56

51   earlier the problem . . . — *Beit Shlomo* to Sh. Ar., HM 132

51   *Israel, my people . . .* — see Hertz, J.H., *A Book of Jewish Thoughts*, p. 54

51   Circumcision — for the basic laws see Yad, *Milah* and Sh. Ar., YD 260–266

53   "Every male . . ." — Gen. 17:10–12

53   Jacob's daughter — Gen. 34:14

53   Moses . . . Zipporah — Ex. 4:25

53   Joshua - Josh. 5:2

54   Queen Jezebel — I Kings 19:14

54   Ezekiel — Ezek. 32:21, 24

54   Jubilees — Book of Jubilees 15:33–34

54   David — Yev. 43b

54   two women . . . babes — II Macc. 6:10

54   Idumeans — Josephus, *Antiquities* 13:157ff

54   Religious leaders — Yev. 46a

54   Rabbi Oshaya — Gen. R. 11:6

55   Paul — Romans 3:4

57   Sabbath — Shab. 130a–132b

58   "Because of the zeal . . . " — Pirkei de Rabbi Eliezer, 29

63   Philo — Philo, *De Circumcisione* 11:210

63   pascal lamb — Ex. 12:48

63   Ezekiel — Ezek. 32:24

63   by that very virtue — Tanḥuma, *Lekh Lekha* (ed. Buber); Ex. R. 19

63   Abraham — Gen. R. 48; see also Gen. R. 46

64   Talmud — Ned. 31b

64   Jeremiah — Jer. 33:25

64   Josephus — Josephus, *Antiquities* 20:2, 3, 4

64   Reform Judaism — Freehof, S., *Reform Responsa* no. 23, 24, 21

65   Spinoza — *Tractatus Theologico–Politicus* (1670), 3:53

65   *Our God . . .* — Prayer Book under Circumcision Ceremony

page

65   Firstborn — for the basic laws see Bek. 2:1, 8:1, 47a—b; Kid. 29a; Yad,
         Bechorim; Sh. Ar., YD 305
66   Inheritance rights — Deut. 21:15—17
66   religious regulations — Ex. 13:11—13
67   Golden Calf — Num. 3:12 and Rashi ad. loc.
70   Egyptian — cf. Ex. 12:12—13, 21—30
70   female firstborns — Sh. Ar., OH 470:1, 2
71   *kohen* and divorcée — Yev. 23a
71   all are female — Sifrei Deut. 215
71   proselyte — Yev. 62a
71   is called her son — Yad, *Naḥalut* 2:12
72   no longer alive — BB 142b
72   *When trouble . . .* — Ta'an. 11a
73   Eliezer — Gen. 15
73   Jacob — Gen. 48:5—6
73   Moses — Ex. 2:10
76   Mordecai — Esth. 2:7, 15
76   Levirate marriage — Gen. 38:8—9; Deut. 15:6
76   Maimonides — Yad, *De'ot* 6:10; for the internal quotes see Ex. 22:21—23 and
         Prov. 22:23
77   "A father . . ." — Ps. 68:6
77   talmudic scholars — Ket. 50a
77   "Happy are they . . . " — Ps. 106:3
78   Guardian — Git. 37a; Responsa Rosh 85:5, 6, 87:1; Sh. Ar., HM 290:1—2
78   minor's father — Responsa Rosh 82:2
79   person and property — *Beit Yosef* to Tur Sh. Ar., HM 290:6; *Isserles* to Sh. Ar.,
         HM 285:8
79   terminate the appointment — Git. 52b
79   death of adopter — Sh. Ar., HM 60:4
79   child's welfare — *Pitḥei Teshuva* to Sh. Ar., EH 82, no. 7
80   "Scripture . . ." — San. 19b; Meg. 13a
80   general tenor . . . document — *Pitḥei Teshuva* to Sh. Ar., EH 19, no. 3
80   non-Jewish child — see Henkin, J., in *Ha-Pardes* vol. 32, no. 4, Jan. 1958
83   *Kaddish* — Moses Sofer to Sh. Ar., OH 164
83   *A woman . . .* — Prov. 31
83   "In the days . . . " — see Hertz, J.H., *A Book of Jewish Thoughts,* p. 11
85   "He who finds . . . " — Prov. 18:22

117

85   "I find the woman . . ." – Ecc. 7:26

85   Rava – Ket. 85a

85   She differs from the man – Kid. 1:7

86   "A careful examination . . . " – Rackman, E., *One Man's Judaism*, p. 330

87   "No amount . . . " – Montefiore, C., *A Rabbinic Anthology*, p. 507

87   reading of the Law – Meg. 23a

90   women acquire merit – Ber. 17a

91   "Let me arise . . . " – Kid. 31b

91   redemption . . . Egypt – Sot. 11b

91   greater faith – Sifrei Num. 133

91   discernment . . . tenderhearted . . . Torah – Nid. 45b; Meg. 14b; Yev. 63b; Ex. R. 41:5

91   Midrash – Gen. R. 18:2; Kid. 49b

94   "Jewish Custom . . ." – see Hertz, J.H., *A Book of Jewish Thoughts*, p. 12

95   *When Israel . . .*   Song R. 4:1

95   "and you shall teach . . . " – Deut. 11:19

95   "Remember the days . . ." – Deut. 32:7

96   Moses – Eruv. 54b

98   "Truly, the name . . . " – BB 21a

99   "If a man have . . . " – Deut. 21:18–21

99   talmudic jurists – San. 8:1, 4, 69b–70a; Yad, *Mamrim* 7:6; Sifrei Deut. 219

99   "there never has . . . " – *Tosefta* San. 11:2

100   "In our times . . . " – Shab. 119b; Edels, *Maharsha* to San. 71a

103   *O my God . . .* – see Hertz, J.H., *A Book of Jewish Thoughts*, p. 18

103   Religious education . . . – Sh. Ar., YD 245–246

104   Jewish law has fixed . . . – Kid. 16b

104   Midrash – Gen. R. 63:10

104   "Moses at Sinai – Rashi to Avot 5:1

107   day of his wedding – *Magen Avraham* to Sh. Ar., OH 225, no. 2

107   talmudic discourse – Luria, S., *Yam Shel Shlomo*, BK 7:37

109   "knowledge about . . . " – Yad, *Edut* 9:8

109   "at five years . . . " – Avot 5:21 as translated by Hertz in *The Authorised Daily Prayer Book*, p. 701, 703

Encyclopedia Judaica, Jerusalem, 1972, under: Abortion, Adoption, Birth, Circumcision, Family, Firstborn, Proselytes, Women.

Epstein, Isidore, *The Jewish Way of Life,* London, 1946.

Feldman, David M., *Birth Control in Jewish Law,* New York, 1968.

Gottlieb, Nathan, *A Jewish Child is Born,* New York, 1960.

Jakobovits, Immanuel, *Jewish Medical Ethics,* New York, 1959.

Loewe, Raphael, *The Position of Women in Judaism,* London, 1966.

Maybaum, Ignaz, *The Jewish Home,* London, 1946.

Patai, Raphael, *Sex and Family in the Bible and Middle East,* Garden City, New York, 1959.

Schauss, Hayyim, *The Lifetime of a Jew Throughout the Ages of Jewish History,* Cincinatti, 1950.

Schlesinger, Benjamin, *The Jewish Family,* Toronto, 1971.

Gerona, Cathedral Archives, *Gerona Apocalypse,* p.5
Mr. B.J. Israel, Bombay, p. 9
London, Library of the British and Foreign Bible Society, p. 11
Photo Alinari, Florence, p. 12, 14
Cambridge, St. John's College Library, p. 13
London, British Museum, p. 16, 71
Groningen, Groningen Museum, p. 18(bottom)
Jerusalem, Yad Vashem Archives, p. 18(top)
Prague, State Jewish Museum, p. 21
Cleveland, O., Joseph B. Horwitz Collection, p. 22
Cecil Roth Photo Collection, p. 23, 68
Jerusalem, A. Bargiora Collection, p. 25
E. Corti, *Die Rothschilds,* Frankfort, 1962, p. 28
P.C. Kirchner, *Juedisches Ceremoniel,* Nuremberg, 1734, p. 36
Tel Aviv, Einhorn Collection, p. 37; color: pl. 6(bottom)
Jerusalem, Folklore Research Center, Hebrew University, p. 39, 78
Amsterdam, Bibliotheca Rosentaliana, p. 40
New York, Jewish Museum, p. 43
New York, Oscar Gruss Collection, p. 45, 52, 84, 97, 100, 102(left), 110; color: pl. 5
Lilienfeld, Abbey Library, *Biblia Pauperum,* p. 47
Jerusalem, M. Atlas Collection, p. 50
Jerusalem, Jewish National and University Library, p. 53
London, Jewish Museum, p. 55
Washington, D.C., National Gallery of Art, p. 56, 75, 89
Photo F. Meyer, Carpentras, p. 58(left)
Rabbi J. Shaw, London, p. 58(right)
Jerusalem, Israel Museum, p. 60; color: pl. 1(top), 2, 3(bottom), 6(top)
New York, Moriah Art-Craft Inc., p. 62
Amsterdam, Stedelijk Museum, p. 64, 66
London, De-Vere Coins Ltd., p. 69(top)
Jerusalem, B.M. Ansbacher Collection, p. 69(bottom)
Kassel, Staatliche Kunstsammlungen, p. 74
New York, Joint Distribution Committee, p. 81
Formerly New York, Zagaysky Collection, p. 82
Formerly London, Arthur Hewitt Collection, p. 86
Challenge, Lubavich Foundation, London, 1970, p. 87
Jerusalem, M. Shalvi Collection, p. 88
Amsterdam, Rijkmuseum, p. 92
Tel Aviv, Haganah Historical Archives, p. 93(top)
Tel Aviv, Israel Government Press Office, p. 93(bottom), 94, 105(top)
H. Hapgood, *The Spirit of the Ghetto,* New York, 1902, p. 102(right)
Jerusalem, Israel State Archives, p. 105(middle)
Jerusalem, Habad Research Center, p. 105(bottom)
Photo Werner Braun, Jerusalem, pl. 1(bottom), 4, 7
En-Harod, Mishkan la-Ommanut, pl. 3(top)
Jerusalem, Sir Isaac and Lady Wolfson Museum, pl. 8
Cover: "The Bar Mitzvah Speech" by Moritz Oppenheim. New York, Oscar Gruss Collection.

120